LETTER WRITING
Made Simple

LETTER WRITING
Made Simple

A GUIDE TO RIGHT COMMUNICATION: BUSINESS AND PERSONAL

MARGARET McCARTHY

JAICO PUBLISHING HOUSE

Ahmedabad Bangalore Chennai
Delhi Hyderabad Kolkata Mumbai

Published by Jaico Publishing House
A-2 Jash Chambers, 7-A Sir Phirozshah Mehta Road
Fort, Mumbai - 400 001
jaicopub@jaicobooks.com
www.jaicobooks.com

Published in arrangement with:
Santa Monica Press, LLC
215 South Highway 101, Suite 110
Solana Beach, CA 92075, USA

To be sold only in India, Bangladesh, Bhutan,
Pakistan, Nepal, Sri Lanka and the Maldives.

LETTER WRITING MADE SIMPLE
ISBN 978-81-8495-996-3

First Jaico Impression: 2017

Printed by
Trinity Academy For Corporate Training Limited, Mumbai

Contents

Author's Note

When I published *Letter Writing Made Easy!* in 1995, I knew I was filling a need among the general public for a clear, easy-to-use guide to writing effective letters. What I didn't know was just how popular the book would be. The response I've received has been very strong and overwhelmingly positive, and I'm deeply gratified that I could have been of such service.

Many have asked me, "When will you write another one? What about this situation, or that occasion?" I had not initially planned a second volume, but after receiving many requests and suggestions, I realized that another volume actually made a lot of sense. Here it is, then: over two hundred new letters for common occasions. I hope you find this second volume of *Letter Writing Made Easy!* as useful as you did the first!

Yours truly,

Margaret McCarthy

Introduction

Though many of us may not like to admit it, sitting down to write a simple letter can be a daunting task. After all, how often does the average person need to use the written word? Phone calls are more common for nearly all types of communication. And even those who have computers and use e-mail find that writing an old-fashioned letter is a more effective form of communication. An e-mail is quick and informal; a letter is more formal, and thus makes a stronger statement. As I said in volume one of *Letter Writing Made Easy!:* "Never underestimate the power of the written word."

Regardless of the content of your message, utilizing a well-written letter makes it "stick" more than any other medium of communication. And after all, what's the point of saying anything unless you want it to really sink in?

As in volume one, the letters provided in this book can be used as is, or embellished with your own personal touch. Sometimes, as in a business letter, this touch will be the addition of your own factual information. Sometimes, as in a personal letter, it will be the addition of your own particular sentiments to a valued friend. Remember, the most effective ingredient in any letter is your own unique spark, that special tone that says "this was written by a distinct personality."

I hope the samples provided here will start you on the path to regularly writing your own powerful letters, smoothly and easily.

Personal Letters

Despite the fact that modern technology has made typing letters easier via word processors and computers, not to mention the fact that these letters can now be faxed or even electronically mailed, there is still nothing more effective than a handwritten personal letter.

Using your own hand conveys intimacy, informality, and a sense of your own style. It leaves no doubt that it was you who wrote it.

Because personal letters contain messages of the utmost importance—after all, there is nothing more important in life than friends and family—they must be worded carefully in order to avoid any possibility of misinterpretation.

With that in mind, here are a few guidelines to writing intimate personal letters.

- Write the date at the top of the first page, but do not include your return address and/or the recipient's address. It is considerate to date a letter to let the recipient know when it was written, but adding the formality of addresses is inappropriate for a personal touch.

- Always greet the recipient using his/her first name. If this seems too informal in a particular circumstance, then you are probably writing a business letter, and should format it as such (see the introduction for business letters).

- After the recipient's first name, use a comma. This is one key distinction between personal and business letters (which use colons). For example, if you are writing to your child's schoolteacher, and your only relationship to her is as her student's parent, then a formal business format is called for, i.e., "**Dear Mrs. Olson:**". On the other hand, if she just happens to be an old, dear friend with whom you are on a first-name basis, then your letter will be handwritten and addressed, "**Dear Mary,**".

• After the salutation, indent the first line of each paragraph.

• Sign off your letter with a close that reflects the nature of your relationship to the recipient, such as "Fondly," "Affectionately," "Love," or "Best regards."

• Use these sample letters as guidelines only. You will notice that most of them get right to the point, avoiding the "small talk" you find in most personal letters. That is because the small talk is up to you. So if you feel more comfortable opening your letter with a few "how are yous" and updates on your personal life, by all means do so. Again, if you team your own common sense with the information here, you'll be writing intimate personal letters in no time!

ONE

Apologies

We all make mistakes. Some are more serious than others, and sometimes it takes friends and loved ones a long time to forgive and forget.

In these cases, a sensitively-written letter is a godsend. It allows you the freedom to gather your thoughts and select your words carefully. Additionally, if the recipient is not ready to speak to you personally, you can convey your message to them without that immediate contact.

In situations in which a long time has passed, a letter is even more appropriate. If you had a "falling out" with a loved one, you don't want to just call him or her out of the blue one day. It is far more appropriate—and respectful—to send a letter. You can choose to break the ice or just open the door a little towards further communication.

One caveat: Never hedge on your apology. Do not say "I am sorry, but I believe I was right. . . " This instantly negates the apology, and defeats your purpose. If you cannot bring yourself to an unqualified apology, then the time is not right for a reconciliation.

In most cases, a well-written letter will open up communication. But if it doesn't, don't beat a dead horse. Just be patient and try again later.

Not Returning Someone's Call/Letter

Dear (**name**),

I feel terrible about taking so long to return your (**call/letter**). Naturally I meant to do it right away, but things have been so hectic with my (**job/kids/ family, etc.**) that it just slipped away from me. I do hope I haven't offended you, or made you think that I don't care. That's not the case at all.

I was very glad to hear from you, and was especially interested in your news about (**event**). I'd like to hear more about it. (**Ask pertinent questions that relate to the event.**)

I'm eager to keep in touch with you, and I'd like us to speak in person soon, if we could. Please call me and let me know when there might be a good time for us to get together. Again, please forgive me for waiting so long to write. I hope to hear from you soon.

Fondly,

Standing Someone Up

Dear (**name**),

It took awhile for me to realize today that I had stood you up for our (**event**) date. When I did realize it, I felt awful. I wish I had a better excuse than to just say "I forgot," but I don't. I've had so many things to deal with that some things have just slipped away from me.

Our (appointment/date/meeting) was one of them.

I can imagine you must be angry at me, and I don't blame you. I would be, too. Will you let me make it up to you? Let's make a new time to have (**breakfast/lunch/dinner**) together, and it will be my treat. Please call me when you have a moment.

Best regards,

An Argument

Dear (**name**),

It's been quite a while since we've spoken. I hope this letter finds you well and happy. I have given a lot of thought to our parting of the ways, and after all this time it still bothers me. Each of us was convinced we were right about (**issue**), and perhaps you still feel as strongly as you did before. However, I don't. After careful thought, I've decided that I would rather have you as my friend than push the point about being "right." I can't take back what I've said, and I can't change my mind completely about what happened. What I'm saying, though, is that I don't want to dwell on what happened any longer. Why does this one argument have to mean that we can't see each other anymore? That seems such a terrible shame. We've shared a lot of good times, and a lot of good conversations. Would you be willing to let bygones be bygones? Please let me know.

Sincerely,

An Inadvertent Slight

Dear (**name**),

I think I owe you an apology. When we were at (**event/place**) (**today/last week, etc.**), I noticed that you seemed upset when I made my remark about (subject). You didn't say anything to me, but I could see you looked disturbed, and I realized you must have been offended by my words.

I'm not sure why my remark had such an effect on you, but I'm truly sorry that it did. You may have heard it differently than I meant; perhaps you think I was implying something more negative or personal than I was. I don't know. All I can say is that your feelings mean a lot to me, and I hate to think that I hurt you. Please accept my apologies, and please know that whatever negative message you heard was definitely not said on purpose. I would never knowingly insult you. I hope you believe that I'm sorry, and that no harm was meant.

I look forward to seeing you or speaking with you again soon.

Warmly,

Missing a Celebration

Dear (**name**),

I just wanted to drop you a note to tell you how sorry I am that I couldn't come to your (**event**). I would have loved to have come, and was hoping I could, but

I found out very close to the time that (**reason why you couldn't attend**). I had to take care of the situation, no matter how much I may have preferred coming to your (**event**). I thought about you all during that day, though, and my warmest wishes were with you. Please accept my apologies, and know that my failure to come wasn't any kind of reflection on how I feel about you.

I heard from (**mutual friend**) that it went beautifully, and that everyone had a good time. I hope it turned out to be everything you hoped for, and that you will continue to include me in future (**event**).

Warmly,

Damaging a Borrowed Object

Dear (**name**),

If I were a dog, I'd be writing this letter to you with my tail tucked between my legs and my head hanging. I'm afraid I have to tell you that I've damaged the (**object**) you lent me. It was just stupidity on my part—I (**describe negligence**), instead of handling it more carefully.

(**If it can be fixed**): The good news is, I think it can be repaired. I looked around and found a place that specializes in these things, and—assuming you're agreeable to this plan—I'll take it there immediately. Naturally I'll pay for the repairs myself.

(**If it can't be fixed**): I don't think there's any hope of saving this particular (**object**), but the good news is that I found a store that specializes in (**object**), and—assuming you're agreeable to this plan—I will buy you a new one immediately.

This is the least I can do for letting you down this way. You were so nice to lend the (**object**) to me, and so friendly about it, and I can't tell you how mad I am at myself for treating your generosity so carelessly. I do hope that my (**repairing/replacing**) it will make up for my mistake.

Sincerely,

Breaking Something During a Visit

Dear (**name**),

I wanted to tell you again how very sorry I was about breaking your (**object**) during (**occasion**) at your house. It was so clumsy of me, and the (**object**) was such a nice one, that I feel terrible. You were very polite about it, which was considerate of you, but I want to make amends. I know the particular (**object**) you had probably can't be replaced exactly, but I would like to pay for my carelessness. Please let me know how much the (**object**) cost, and I will be more than happy to send you a check. Please accept my offer—it's the least I can do.

Sincerely,

Not Acknowledging an Achievement

Dear (**name**),

It's already been several (**days/weeks/months**) since your (**achievement**) and I'm ashamed to see that I've let so much time go by without saying a word.

You worked long and hard for the (**achievement**), and you richly deserve the accolades you've earned. I'm happy and excited for you, and of course, very proud. I deeply admire your seemingly endless talent and energy. Congratulations many times over, and please forgive my lapse in manners for not saying so sooner.

Love,

Fighting About Religion or Politics

Dear (**name**),

I'm writing to say how sorry I am that we fought in our last conversation. You know, they say that religion and politics are the two subjects you should never discuss—and now I know why! It's so tempting to get carried away and push a point you feel strongly about. And of course, not having really gone into this with you before, I didn't realize how much our ideas differ. So the surprise of learning that you believe things so opposite to my own beliefs made me especially feisty, and I feel that I let my arguing get out of hand.

Why don't we just agree to disagree, and let things stand at that? I respect your right to your own opinion, as I'm sure you respect mine. It will probably be healthier and easier to avoid (**subject**) in the future. After all, we've got plenty of other things that we share and can talk about happily! I hope you'll agree to put that unpleasant argument behind us, and move on. I look forward to talking to you again soon.

Warmly,

Turning Down a Birthday Invitation

Dear (**name**),

Thank you very much for sending me an invitation to your upcoming birthday party. I was excited by the prospect of going, but when I checked the date against my calendar, I realized that I had a previous commitment. I'd much rather go to your party, but I can't get out of this other event.

How about celebrating on our own another time? Are you available (**day or date**)? I'd love to take you out to lunch or a movie, or do something else that you might like. Birthdays are fun, and I'd hate to pass up celebrating yours this year, just because of a conflict of dates. Please let me know how and when I can make it up to you.

Love,

Turning Down a Wedding Invitation

Dear (**name**),

I was delighted to receive your wedding invitation, but when I checked the date against my calendar, I realized that I had a previous commitment. I'd much rather go to your wedding, but I can't get out of this other event.

I am so happy that you and (**name of fiancee**) have decided to spend the rest of your lives together. I'm sure everyone is drowning you in their congratulations these days, but I hope you know how heartfelt my happiness is for you and (**name of fiancee**).

Even though I can't be there to witness the event, I'll definitely be there in spirit. I'm also sending along a gift for you and (**name of fiancee**); I hope you'll like it. Congratulations again, and may you both have a long and happy life together.

With love,

Pet's Destruction of Property

Dear (**name**),

I want to apologize for the damage my (**type of pet**) did to your (**object**). It's annoying enough when your own animal does something like this, but to have to take it from someone else's pet is even more irritating. I'm sorry you had to experience that. I wish I could have done something to prevent this from happening, but I guess a little unpredictability from (**type of pet**) is to be expected. After all, they *are* animals.

Anyway, I'd like very much to (**repair/replace**) your (**object**). Please let me know how much it will cost, and I will write you a check immediately. If you'd like me to take care of the details in getting it (**repaired/replaced**), I'd be more than happy to do this. Thanks for your understanding, and please accept my apologies once again.

Sincerely,

Bounced Check

Dear (**name**),

I was very surprised, and distressed, to learn that the check I wrote you for (**occasion**) bounced. Believe me, I would never have written it if I had thought there weren't sufficient funds to cover it. The only thing that can explain this is that either I miscalculated my balance, or else a check I deposited took longer to clear than I expected. Whatever the reason, it shouldn't have happened, and I apologize. I'm enclosing a money order for the full amount, as well as (**amount**) to cover any service charges you might have incurred from your bank. I hope this will clear up the problem, and again, my apologies.

Sincerely,

Child's Carelessness

Dear (**name**),

My (**son/daughter**) came home after visiting your house and told me, very sadly, that (**he/she**) had accidentally damaged (**your/your child's object**). It was very nice of you not to bring it up yourself, but of course I insist on (**repairing/replacing**) it. My (**son/daughter**) would like that, too.

Please let me know how much it will cost, and I will write you a check immediately. If you'd like me to take care of the details in getting it (**repaired/replaced**), I'd be more than happy to do this. Thanks for your understanding, and please accept my apologies for this unfortunate accident.

Thank you,

Revealed Secret

Dear (**name**),

I have to tell you something that's a little difficult for me to discuss. I did something accidentally the other day that will probably upset you—I was having a conversation with (**person**), and we got onto the subject of (**subject**). Somehow, without even realizing what I was doing, I heard myself say that you (**secret information**). As soon as the words came out of my mouth, I regretted saying them. This was information that you asked me not to repeat, and I can't believe I broke your confidence like that. It is really not like me, and I can guarantee you it has never happened before, and will not happen again.

That's not a consolation to you, I'm sure. But I want you to know, first of all, that I have not told anyone else; this was the only time I have ever mentioned (**subject**). Also, I wanted you to hear it from me first, so that it wouldn't come back to you through the grapevine.

I am terribly sorry about this, and very angry at myself for being so stupid. I hope no negative repercussions come from this. I won't blame you if you're angry at me, but all I can say in my own defense is that it was genuinely an accident. I had no intention of hurting you, and I'm very disappointed in myself if that's what I've done. Please let me know if you can forgive me for this.

Sincerely,

TWO

Condolences and Sad Occasions

In a time of tragedy, it is natural to respect the privacy of a loved one and simply step aside. The fact that it is extremely difficult to find the right words to convey sympathy and condolence only add to the challenge of doing—and saying—the right thing.

So a letter is the perfect solution. It is not imposing, and it allows you the freedom to choose your words carefully, which, under the circumstances, is optimal.

Brevity is highly recommended—again, a lengthy letter may seem too imposing in a time of grief. It is appropriate, however, to express support and share a fond memory. This will gently ease the recipient's burden and make he or she feel less alone. And when the grieving period is over, your gesture will long be remembered and appreciated.

it isn't necessarily a reflection on you as a student or as a person. There are many other schools out there that have great reputations, where you could be very happy, and I hope you'll look into them.

If you really have your heart set on (**name of college**), you could always ask them how you might improve your application, and then reapply next year. Sometimes colleges accept return applicants. Either way, I hope you can put this in the proper perspective and move forward with your college plans. You've got a great future ahead of you, and this doesn't need to be a serious roadblock for you. I know you'll eventually get into a good school, and do very well once there. I'm rooting for you!

Best,

Fired (Co-Worker)

Dear (**name**),

When I heard that (**name of boss**) had let you go, I was really surprised and sad. I don't know the details of your firing, but I've always thought you did a great job here. You've certainly made my workdays more pleasant; I've enjoyed having (**coffee breaks/lunch, etc.**) with you. You've got a lot of talent, and I'm sure you'll find something else soon. Let me know if I can put in a good word for you, okay? And please keep in touch; I'd like to know how you're doing. I'll miss you!

Good luck,

Fired (Friend)

Dear (**name**),

I was shocked to hear your news about being let go from your job, and I want you to know you have my total sympathy and support. Based on what you told me about (**name of company**), it sounds like they do not have very good managerial skills. I can't believe they'd be so dumb as to let you go. Who knows what they were thinking. I'm really sorry you have to go through this; I know how depressing it can be. But remember, there are lots of other jobs out there, and any number of places that would appreciate you more than (**name of company**) did.

I'd be happy to ask around for you, if you so desire. Just let me know. In the meantime, try to look on the bright side: you've got some "down time" now, so while you're job-hunting, give yourself a little time to relax and enjoy life before joining the rat race again.

Hang in there, and let me know if I can be of any help.

Best regards,

Financial Difficulties

Dear (**name**),

I just wanted to let you know how sorry I was to hear about your recent financial setbacks. I understand how stressful it can be to have debts piling up, and to bc hit with an unexpected shortage of cash. Just so you know, I'd be happy to lend you some money if you need it. And before you say no because you're too proud to accept gifts, let me tell you that it wouldn't be a gift. I'd expect it back, and we could fix whatever kind of terms with which you're comfortable. I'm not rich, but I could lend you a hand, and I'd be more than happy to help you. All you have to do is let me know. I'm also here, of course, if you just need a friendly ear or sounding board.

Warmly,

Failure of Enterprise

Dear (**name**),

I was sad to hear about the failure of your (**type of enterprise**); I know this outcome isn't what you'd hoped for. It wasn't what I'd hoped for, either—your enthusiasm and hard work were very inspirational and I was really rooting for you.

All I can say is that nothing is ever a wasted experience. You're an extremely dedicated and talented person, and I know you can learn from this and move on to an even brighter project. There's no question that you have it in you to succeed, and if you keep trying, I know it will happen for you. Please try not to let this disappointment hold you back. You've got a fan in me, and I'll always be here to cheer you on and to help you in anyway possible.

Warmly,

Surgery

Dear (**name**),

I'm so sorry to hear about the necessity of your upcoming surgery. Surgery is a frightening prospect, but I hear you've got a good doctor, and I know you'll come through this with flying colors. All of your family and friends are rooting for you. Keep your chin up...and try not to eat too much of that hospital food! I'll come and visit you as often as I can. And please do not hesitate to let me know if there's anything in particular I can bring for you.

Best,

Serious Illness

Dear (**name**),

I was so sorry to hear about your (**type of illness**). It must have come as a tremendous shock to you. Just remember to keep your thoughts positive throughout all of this; it will make your (**recovery/rehabilitation**) that much easier. Try to focus on getting better.

Please know that I'm here to help in any way that I can. I'm willing to help you take care of any details that may arise, or to just come visit you if you want some company. All you have to do is let me know.

My thoughts and my prayers are with you.

Love,

Terminal Illness

Dear (**name**),

Words cannot express how devastated I was to hear of your recent diagnosis. I have been wanting to speak to you so badly, but every time I tried to muster the courage to call, I pulled back for fear that you might not be ready to talk about your (**type of illness**) yet. Please don't think that my not contacting you until now means that I don't care. I care deeply, and want to give you all the support that I can.

I understand fully what this turn of events means, but I can't help clinging to some optimism through it all. New treatments and even cures are being developed all the time, and I have to believe that one may be able to help you. Please don't give up hope. And please call on me any time if I can bring you any help or comfort. I think of you and pray for you daily.

Love,

Miscarriage

Dear (**name**),

I just wanted to let you know how sad I was to hear about your loss. It must have been a great disappointment for you and (**name of father/mother**). I'm sure you've heard from your doctor, and from other friends, how very common it is to lose a fetus in the first weeks of a pregnancy. Many people in your situation have gone on to successfully conceive and have children, and I'm sure that can happen for you, too. I hope that thought can sustain you through this difficult time. If you need to talk, please don't hesitate to call on me. I'm keeping you and (**name of father/mother**) in my prayers.

Love,

Convalescing Co-Worker

Dear (**name**),

Hopefully, by the time you get this card, you'll be feeling much better after your (**illness/accident**). All of us here at the office have been missing you, and hoping your recovery is speeding along. Please don't hesitate to let me or anyone else in the office know if there's something around here that you need taken care of while you're recovering. We're all just a phone call away. Meanwhile, take good care of yourself so you can come back soon.

Best wishes,

Victim of a Crime

Dear (**name**),

What a shock to learn that you were (**nature of crime**). It's hard to understand how cruel people can be, and how such cruelty continues to flourish. You must be feeling very disoriented and angry, and I want you to know how sorry I am for the terrible anxiety this must be causing you. My only solace is that you are (**unharmed/alive**). I hope that you and the police are successful in tracking down whoever did this to you, and in the meantime, please let me know if there's anything at all that I can do to help you through this difficult period.

Best wishes,

Marriage or Relationship Difficulties

Dear (**name**),

When you told me that you and (**name of spouse/significant other**) were having trouble, it wasn't a complete surprise. You haven't been happy for a while, and no one can hide their unhappiness all the time. Still, it made me sad for you, and I wanted you to know how sorry I am that you're going through this difficult time.

I also want to make it clear, in case you don't know already, that although (**name of spouse/significant other**) is a nice person whom I like a great deal, you are my primary friend. If you need a shoulder to cry on, or just someone to talk to, I want you to know that I'm here for you. I'm keeping my hopes up that the two of you can work things out. And no matter what, I will always be your friend.

Love,

Recent Breakup

Dear (**name**),

I know you're going through a terrible time right now, trying to adjust to your recent breakup with (**name of significant other**). Although my heart goes out to you, a part of me is also convinced that you deserve a lot better, and that you shouldn't mourn the loss of (**name of significant other**) for very long.

I put this on paper so that you can take it out and look at it, and remind yourself that you are clearly the superior person in this scenario, and that (**name of significant other**), while very nice in some ways, is not the right mate for you. You are a beautiful person with a lot to offer; as the old saying goes, there are plenty of fish in the sea. And if you keep yourself in the "swim" of things, you'll find that another, better, and more *deserving* fish will swim right up to you very soon.

Love,

Cancellation of Wedding

Dear (**name**),

Regretfully, I have to tell you that (**name of fiancee**) and I have decided to call off our wedding. It wasn't an easy decision to make, but it's the best decision for both of us. I'm returning the gift you sent, with thanks for your generosity. I hope this change in plans doesn't cause you too much inconvenience.

Thank you,

Informing Family and Friends of Divorce

Dear (**names**),

I'm sorry to have to tell you this, but (**name of spouse**) and I have decided to get a divorce. This may not be a total surprise to you, given how tense things have been between us as of late. We've spent a lot of time discussing this, and the decision is final. I don't really want to go into details at this point; I just wanted to give you the facts, and we can talk more about it when things settle down. As of (**date**), (**I/name of spouse**) will be moving out. (**If you are the one moving**): My new address and phone number are included below. Thank you for your support during this difficult time.

Love,

Goodbye to Ex-Significant Other's Family

Dear (**names**),

I'm sure by now that (**ex-significant other's name**) has told you that (**he/she**) and I are no longer a couple. Before I disappear from your life entirely, I wanted to thank you. I've spent many memorable times with you over the past (**number of months/years**), and you've always been so wonderful to me, that I couldn't just fade away without a goodbye. I'm truly grateful to you for always making me feel welcome, and for treating me like a part of your family. I'll miss that.

I hope (**you/both of you/all of you**) are well, and that you'll remember the good times we shared with as much fondness as I do. Thanks again for everything.

Sincerely,

To Child on Rejection from Sports Team or Performance Group

Dear (**name**),

It's always a bitter disappointment to want to join something and be told you can't. I've been there myself, so I know. I'm sure you're feeling bad about not making the (**type of team/group**), but I wanted to tell you that you shouldn't get too discouraged about this. Even though it may not seem like it right now, there will be other (**type of teams/groups**) in your future, and if you persevere, you'll be a part of one of them. This just may not have been the right time for you.

You have talent *and* enthusiasm, two very important gifts, and I know it won't be long before you find a (**type of team/group**) that will appreciate these qualities. You're a terrific person, and always will be, regardless of this minor setback. Don't stop trying, and remember that you are a very valuable human being.

Love,

To Child on Fight with Friend

Dear (**name**),

I was sorry to hear that you had a fight with (**friend's name**). I know how painful that can be. Just remember, the ill feeling between you and (**friend's name**) will not last forever. If you wait until your feelings calm down, (**his/her**) feelings will probably have calmed down too. Then you can try to patch things up. Remember that it's always better to say "I'm sorry" and still have your friend, than refusing to apologize and losing someone dear to you. I hope you can make up soon, so that you can go back to being friends again.

Good luck,

Setback in College

Dear (**name**),

I was sorry to hear about the setback you experienced in school this term. I know college can be an overwhelming experience—there are so many different responsibilities and different activities that must be juggled. Part of what you learn from it all is how to manage your time and resources—a skill with which nobody is born. And in the process of learning, there will always be a few mishaps, a few disappointing events.

I sincerely hope that you can keep your attitude positive, and try not to be too hard on yourself. You're doing very well with a new set of tough challenges, and I know you'll find a clear path through the thorns. You have my support and, if you want it, my advice—but I'll wait until you ask. The bottom line is, you're my (**friend/niece/nephew, etc.**), and I'll always be proud of you, and I'll always be here for you.

Love,

THREE

Encouragement

The following letters are examples of writing from the heart, either expressing genuine support for a loved one's pending challenge, communicating honest emotions, or simply telling someone you are thinking of them.

This type of thought is often communicated verbally, and that's a shame, because the message will contain an even greater value if it is written. The key is to offer your emotional support genuinely, but realistically. Don't make promises that you can't keep, because in the long run, that will do more harm than good. A combination of a generous spirit and a pragmatic approach is ideal.

Becoming a Single Parent

Dear (**name**),

You've probably been getting some flak from certain people—like your (**mother/father/priest, etc.**)!—since you announced that you were going have a child on your own. Well, I just wanted to stand up and be counted among the people who support you. Your decision takes real courage, and I know you wouldn't have made it if you didn't feel equal to the challenge. You've got enough love and common sense for two parents, and I'm sure your baby will thrive with you.

There are so many ways a single parent can get help these days, from daycare to child-friendly workplaces, that I'm sure you'll be able to make it work. Also, as you know, I'm here for you too. Any time I can give you a hand with something, just let me know.

Good for you, (**name**), and may God bless both you and your baby.

Love,

To Student Preparing for Difficult Exams

Dear (**name**),

I know you've got some tough exams coming up, and I just wanted to write you a note to say "I know you can do it!" The one thing you really have to watch out for is stress. It's so easy to fall into the trap of being too hard on yourself, and thinking that the whole world depends on these exams. Please remember, (**name**), that "important" isn't the same as "life or death." Try not to put too much pressure on yourself: just focus your energies, work sensible hours, and get plenty of sleep. You're such a smart young (**woman/man**) that I have no doubt you'll do very well. Good luck!

Love,

To Child Starting a New School

Dear (**name**),

This is a "good luck" message for you, since you'll be starting your new school very soon. I know that leaving your old school and your old friends was sad for you, but you'll have a terrific time at your new school, too.

The first couple of days might be hard as you get used to your new surroundings, but soon you'll see that the other kids will be wanting to get to know "the new kid on the block." Just be the wonderful (**boy/girl**) that you are, and I guarantee things will go well. I'm looking forward to hearing how you like your new school, so give me a call or write me a note after you're settled in. Remember, I'll be rooting for you!

Love,

Going Back to School

Dear (**name**),

I just wanted to tell you that I think it's really fantastic that you decided to go back to school. It takes courage and commitment to make such a decision when you're past the "normal" age of most college students, and you've got plenty of both. I know it's going to be a fun and highly rewarding experience for you.

I also think you'll find that there are plenty of other folks your age—and older—returning to school so that you will have a peer group of your own, and you won't feel lost in a sea of sorority and fraternity kids! Once again, congratulations and good luck. I'm behind you one hundred percent!

Sincerely,

Embarking on an Important Business Trip

Dear (**name**),

Well, you're off to (**location**), and I just wanted to let you know that I'm sure you'll do great! I know this is an important trip for you, and that a lot is riding on the outcome. You've got everything you need to do well, and in addition to your own gifts, you'll be taking along the good wishes and warm thoughts of everyone who loves you. Think positive, and you'll do fine. And try to have a little fun while you're there, too! See you when you get home.

Love,

Starting Own Business

Dear (**name**),

When you told me about the (**type of business**) you planned to start, I was a little worried at first, because it's so hard to get a new enterprise off the ground. But the more I think about it, the better it sounds. This idea is perfect for you...you have all the qualities a person needs for this kind of project.

I'm really excited for you, and also extremely proud of you for implementing your ideas in this manner. I know you'll succeed, and I wanted to tell you that you have my support and my best wishes. I look forward to seeing your (**store/finished product, etc.**) and I promise I'll be one of your first (**customers/subscribers, etc.**)!

Sincerely,

To a Colleague After a Setback

Dear (**name**),

I know you've had a hard time lately because of the (**nature of setback**) you had here at work. I've been thinking about you, and I just wanted to say, "keep your chin up."

I know this feels like a disappointment, but there are so many opportunities here, so many types of problems or events that come up, that you're going to have a lot of other chances to shine. This isn't really as big a deal as it may seem right now. Sometimes things don't go as well as expected; other times, it'll be your turn to succeed. I know that time will come soon, and until then, just remember that you are an important part of what we do here, and I for one am in your corner.

Best,

Maintaining Friendships After a Breakup

Dear (**name**),

It's been awhile since we last spoke, and as you've probably heard, (**name of significant other**) and I have broken up. Since you and (**name of significant other**) were friends long before I came onto the scene, it has occurred to me that my friendship with you might be affected by our breakup.

I just want to let you know that I hope this doesn't happen. I've always enjoyed your company and genuinely like you. If you feel the same way about me, there's no reason we need to lose each other's friendship because of what's happened between (**name of significant other**) and me.

I'm not asking you to take any sides; I don't even think we need to ever discuss the breakup. You and I have always had plenty of other things to talk about, and have always enjoyed each other's company, and I don't see why we can't continue to do so. Please let me know what you think. I wouldn't want you to do anything that makes you uncomfortable, but I also hate to lose good friends.

Warmly,

To Friend Who is Taking Care of Someone Who is Ill/Injured

Dear (**name**),

I just wanted to drop you a line to let you know how supportive I am of your efforts to help (**name of ill/injured person**). I know it's a hard job, and often a very sad one, and I think that you're a wonderful person for taking the burden onto yourself. You may think it was the "obvious" thing to do, but believe me, there are some people out there who wouldn't make that sacrifice, no matter what the circumstances. You truly have my admiration.

I also want you to know that I'm here for you. If you need a hand running errands or just need a little emotional support, please don't hesitate to call. I know you're doing a good job taking care of (**name of ill/injured person**)—just don't forget to take good care of yourself as well.

Love,

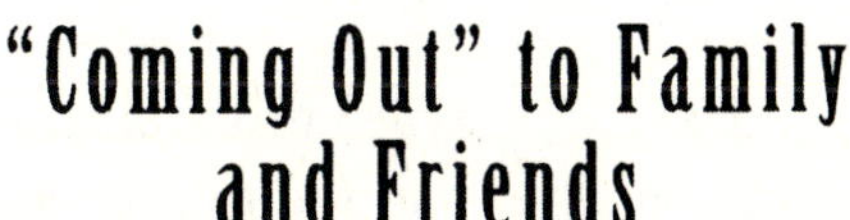

"Coming Out" to Family and Friends

Dear (**name**),

I can only imagine how difficult it was for you to make your announcement last (**night/week/month, etc.**). I know you've probably received a mixed reaction from your friends and family, but I just wanted to write this note to tell you how completely supportive and proud of you I am. Making a statement of identity like that—especially one that's still, unfortunately, controversial—isn't easy. I'm very inspired by how brave and resolute you were, and I dearly hope that your honesty is being rewarded by the people you told.

You are very special to me, and now that I know how brave you are, I value you even more. You will never receive anything but affection and acceptance from me, and I wish you no less from every other person in your life.

Love,

Training for Athletic Event

Dear (**name**),

I just wanted to drop you a note to say how impressed I am with the long hours and hard work you are putting in training for (**type of athletic event**). I find it extremely inspiring to think of your tremendous effort and commitment. I'm sure you must get tired sometimes, or maybe even feel negative about your chances on a bad day. But take it from someone who's an objective observer: you've got all the talent and drive to do a beautiful job, and if anyone can excel at (**type of athletic event**), you can. I'm rooting for you all the way! Good luck, and remember to have fun.

Best wishes,

FOUR

Congratulations

Many people simply buy pre-written greeting cards for these occasions. Although this practice has become acceptable in our society, it pales in comparison to a personal message that is written by you.

Achievements are important—and sometimes rare—moments in people's lives, and they should be honored accordingly. The following letters are designed for most congratulatory occasions, and can be either handwritten on your stationery or on a blank greeting card.

Adopting a Child

Dear (**name**),

I was happy to hear that you and (**name of spouse/significant other**) have become parents! I've been rooting for you for so long. I know how disappointing and frustrating it was for you to have to wait so many (**months/years**). But the long wait has finally paid off, and now your own (**son/daughter**) is at home with you! I can only imagine how happy you both must be right now.

That little (**boy/girl**) is very lucky—(**he/she**) doesn't know it yet, but (**he/she**)'s going to grow up with two of the nicest people in the world as parents. I've always felt sure you would make wonderful parents, and I can't tell you how glad I am that you finally have a chance to pass along your warmth and good sense to a child. Congratulations, and much love.

Best wishes,

Conceiving a Child

Dear (**name**),

I was thrilled to learn that you and (**name of spouse/significant other**) are expecting (**another/your first**) child! I know you've been wanting to become parents (**again/for some time**), and it looks like you've been blessed. I can only imagine how happy you both must be right now.

This child is very lucky—(**he/she**) doesn't know it

yet, but (**he/she**)'s going to grow up with two of the warmest and most loving people in the world as parents. Congratulations, and much love.

Best wishes,

Losing Weight

Dear (**name**),

Over the past (**number of weeks/months**) I've noticed that you've been gradually slimming down, and I thought it looked very becoming on you. But it wasn't until you told me how much you'd lost that I realized just what an accomplishment this is for you!

(**Number**) pounds is a lot of weight and I'm extremely impressed and proud of you. I'm sure it's been a tough road sometimes, but the results are worth it. You look wonderful, and you've shown yourself and others that you really have the perseverance to stick to something difficult and see it through. Good for you! I hope you feel as good as you look, and that you're able to enjoy this success for a long time to come.

Best,

Leaving a Bad Situation

Dear (**name**),

I was surprised to hear that you've decided to leave your (**significant other/job, etc.**). Surprised, but also relieved. I know that for some time you've been struggling with this decision, and I also know that it's caused you a lot of grief.

For a long time now, every time you've mentioned (**name of significant other/job, etc.**), you've had mostly negative things to say. I've often wished you weren't involved with something that made you so unhappy, but you had to make that decision for yourself. I'm very glad that you've finally taken the initiative. There's a whole world of opportunities out there for you, and I'm positive you can find a situation that will bring you a lot more satisfaction than this one has. Congratulations on making a hard, but definitely correct, choice.

Fondly,

Embarking on a Vacation

Dear (**name**),

Finally, you're going away on a vacation! You've worked awfully hard, and for a very long stretch, and you really deserve this time for yourself. When you told me you were going to (**location**) I was immediately jealous. Do you think you could fit me in your suitcase? Probably not...but at least send me some postcards so I can see how nice it is there. And if you need me to take care of anything while you are away, please do not hesitate to ask. I look forward to hearing about your adventures when you return.

Bon voyage,

To Child on Appearance in School Performance

Dear (**name**),

I just wanted to tell you how much I enjoyed coming to the (**type of performance**) and seeing you on stage! You were wonderful. Even though it was a group effort, and many children took part in the production, you stood out—I could hardly take my eyes off you! I especially liked the part where you (**describe activity**). I had a lot of fun seeing the (**type of performance**), and I hope you had a lot of fun being in it, too. Congratulations!

Love,

To Child on Earning High Grades

Dear (**name**),

I just heard about the report card you got last (**week/month/semester**), and I'm amazed. All those wonderful grades! I know how much time it takes to earn good grades, so you must have been working very hard. I'm so proud of you, and your parents are, too. If you keep doing such terrific work, you're going to have a very bright, successful future. Now you've earned some time off, so enjoy your (**winter/summer/spring**) vacation. Give yourself a treat and have fun! You've earned it.

Love,

To Child on Acceptance to Sports Team or Performance Group

Dear (**name**),

Your (**mom/dad/uncle, etc.**) just told me that you tried out for (**name of team/group**) and were accepted! I think that's wonderful. I know you have a lot of hard work ahead of you, because you'll have to practice after school and then still handle your homework and chores—but I also know you'll have a lot of fun. Since you love (**type of activity**) so much, it will be a great experience for you. I can't wait to see you in a (**game/performance, etc.**)!

Love,

To Child on Winning Competition

Dear (**name**),

How wonderful it is that you've won the (**type of competition**)! I know you were working very hard toward that goal, and all of your (**practice/preparation**) paid off. It feels good when that happens, doesn't it? I hope you managed to have fun despite all of the nervousness and hard work. I'm really proud of you, and I know your parents are, too. I've always known you were a gifted young (**man/woman**), and now everyone else knows it too. Congratulations!

Love,

Co-Worker's Accomplishment

Dear (**name**),

Congratulations on your (**describe accomplishment**). I have to admit that when you first began this project, I was a little skeptical that it could be accomplished, or accomplished so well. But I'm happy to say that you really proved me wrong! You were the perfect (**man/woman**) for the job, and the results couldn't have been better. By (**describe accomplishment**) you've helped the entire (**company/business/store, etc.**). We're very lucky to have you!

Best wishes,

Achieving Professional Success

Dear (**name**),

I just wanted to add my congratulations to the long list of such wishes I'm sure you've been receiving lately. It's quite a coup you accomplished at work—you did a wonderful job with (**describe project**), and I'm glad to hear that your (**colleagues/boss**) have noticed and appreciated your fine work. I'm very impressed that you're so able to apply your talent and skills to this job, and come up with such first-rate results. I'm very proud of you, as I'm sure your other friends and family are, too. Congratulations!

Warmly,

FIVE

Special Occasions

These days, perhaps the highest number of written messages we send are for special occasions. Most of us simply buy pre-written greeting cards for these purposes, but it need not be so. You can either create your own card, write a nice note on your stationery, or write your message on a blank card.

In any case, most of these messages are highly personal, and so these samples are, by necessity, only suggestions. Whenever possible, you should write from your own heart. Use the following samples as a guideline.

To Parents of Child's Fiancee, Upon Engagement

Dear (**names**),

What wonderful news we've received from our kids! (**Spouse's name**) and I are thrilled that (**your child's name**) and (**their child's name**) have decided to get married, and we're sure you are, too. Your (**son/daughter**) is a wonderful person, and we're delighted that (**he/she**) will be a member of our family.

We should probably talk about wedding plans, and what sort of gifts we'd like to give to the kids. Perhaps we could meet or speak soon? Please give us a call and let us know when we might be able to get together. We're looking forward to hearing from you, and welcome you and (**their child's name**) to our family. Congratulations to all of us!

Best,

Goodbye to Colleague

Dear (**name**),

It's been a real pleasure working with you over the last (**length of time**). You've brought so much to our work environment here, and you'll truly be missed. No one else can ever possibly hope to replace you! I hope your new job at (**name of company**) turns out to be fun, exciting and extremely fulfilling. Our loss will certainly be their gain.

Best wishes,

Goodbye When Moving Away

Dear (**name**),

It's not easy to say goodbye to someone whose company I've enjoyed as much as yours. Even though I'm excited to be moving to (**name of city/state/country**), and starting a new life there, it makes me very sad to think of not living near you anymore.

I just wanted to write this note to tell you how great it's been knowing you, and that I still want to keep in touch with you after the move. For the record, here's my new address and phone number (**include information**). Of course I know where to find you! Thanks for some great times, and please keep in touch.

Goodbye,

To Child on Religious Rite of Passage

Dear (**name**),

You have a big day coming up—your (**confirmation/Bar Mitzvah/Bat Mitzvah, etc.**)! What a wonderful time for you. You must be very excited to be making this important step in your life. I know you have a lot of preparation to do, and I'm sure you're taking care of your duties. When the day finally arrives, I know you'll be well-prepared and will make all of us very proud. I can't wait to see you on your special day. Good luck!

Love,

Anniversary of Dating

Dear (**name**),

It's hard to believe that it's been (**number of months/years**) since we've been dating. The time I've spent with you has gone by so fast; I guess I must really be enjoying myself! I can't tell you how much you've brought into my life; you've given me things I never knew I was missing, but which I couldn't possibly live without anymore. Thank you for changing my life so positively, and for loving me so much. I hope we're together for a long time to come. Happy anniversary, (**name of significant other**).

Love,

Birth of Grandchild

Dear (**name**),

Congratulations on the birth of your grandchild! What wonderful news. You and your family must be very happy. Being a (**grandma/grandpa**) is the best of both worlds: You get to enjoy the fun of playing with a baby and watching (**him/her**) grow, without the responsibilities or the burdens of actually raising (**him/her**). And you get to be very popular with the child, because it'll be your job to spoil (**him/her**) rotten! May you and your new (**grandson/granddaughter**) have years of joy ahead of you.

Best wishes,

SIX

Thank-You Notes

Too often in a situation that calls for a thank-you note, we simply take the lazy way out and send a pre-written card. In fact, a handwritten thank-you note is far more effective, and shows that you since you took the time to write it, your appreciation is genuine. Once again, adding your own personal touches to the following samples is always a good idea.

Thank You for Taking Care of Our House While We Were Away

Dear (**name**),

What a godsend you've been! It was so wonderful to come home (**last night/last week, etc.**), exhausted from our trip and all the traveling, and find the house looking so beautiful. We especially appreciated the way you (**describe what they did**). Thank you very, very much.

We're grateful to you for helping out. In fact, we brought you a little something from our travels to (**name of place**) as a token of our gratitude. We'd love to see you soon to give it to you. Please give us a call so we can set up a time to get together. And please, if you ever need us to return this favor, don't hesitate to ask.

Fondly,

Support During Crisis

Dear (**name**),

As you know, this has been a very trying time for me. I just want to tell you how valuable your help has been. Your willingness to listen, to offer advice, and to just give me a shoulder to cry on, has meant more to me than you will ever know. You are an incredibly good friend. I hope I can do something for you one day that will help you as much as you've helped me.

Love,

Helping Us Move

Dear (**name**),

I know I already said "thanks," but after what we all went through the other day, I think a written thank-you is definitely in order. What a big job that was! You were terrific, coming out to help us and pitching in so completely. We couldn't have finished as soon as we did without your help. You're a really good friend to do something so demanding for us—thank you very, very much. If and when you ever move, we want to be the first people you call for help.

Warmly,

Watching the Kids

Dear (**name**),

When I was called away the other day, I didn't know what I would do with my (**son/daughter/kids**). It was so unexpected when I found out I had to go to (**place**), I had no time to call my usual babysitters.

Frankly, when I asked if you could watch them, I didn't expect that you'd be able to do so at the last minute like that. I was so relieved when you said yes! And best of all, my (**son/daughter/kids**) said (**he/she/they**) had a great time with you. You really came through for me—thank you very, very much. Please let me know if you ever need help with something. Last minute or not, I promise I'll be there for you.

Thanks again,

To Clergy for Meaningful Service

Dear (**Rabbi/Pastor/Father, etc.**),

I just wanted to let you know that the service you led last (**day/date/occasion**) was truly a revelation. The points you raised about (**issue**) made me think of aspects in my life in a different way, and gave me some new insights into my daily existence.

I especially appreciated the portion when you said (**describe highlight of service**). I enjoy all of your sermons, but this one was particularly meaningful to me, and I wanted to thank you for the eloquence and insight you brought to it.

Best wishes,

To Clergy for Helpful Counsel

Dear (**Rabbi/Pastor/Father, etc.**),

The past several (**days/weeks, etc.**) have been very difficult for me as I've struggled with (**describe problem**). Speaking to you the other day was very helpful in resolving this issue for me; you gave me a lot to think about, and your words were very comforting.

I realize this is all in a day's work for you, but your kindness and generosity with your time truly impressed me. You've made a big difference in my feelings and outlook, and I'm extremely grateful. Thank you for all of your wisdom and good will.

Warmly,

To Co-Worker Who Helped You

Dear (**name**),

Thank you for all of the help you gave me on (**project**). I was floundering a little at first, and when I asked you for some help, you were extremely gracious and nice about it. Without your (type of help) I never could have gotten the project off the ground.

Although (**name of boss**) singled me out for praise on this project, I want you to know that I went to (**him/her**) and told (**him/her**) that your help was invaluable. (**He/she**) seemed pleased to know this. Giving you the credit you deserve is the least I could do; please let me know if I can ever return the favor by giving you a hand if you should need it.

Thanks,

Help with Project

Dear (**name**),

This is just to thank you for the assistance you gave me with (**describe project**). There was a lot to do, and not much time to do it in, and your pitching in made ali the difference. It was really great of you to offer your time like that. If I can ever help you out with something, just let me know and I'll be there ASAP.

Thanks again,

To Childhood Teacher

Dear (**name**),

I'll bet you're either surprised to hear from me, or else you don't remember who I am. Well, I'm (**name**) and I was your student in (**class and year**) at (**school**). It's been a few years, hasn't it? The reason I'm writing is to tell you how big an influence you had on me. I didn't realize it at the time, but you played an important part in the shaping of my character. I especially remember (**explain memories**) and how you taught me that (**explain what you learned**).

You hear so many negative things about education these days; no one seems to be mentioning all of the good teachers out there. You are definitely one of the good ones, and I wanted you to know that I'm grateful. I'll never forget you, (**name**). Thanks for everything.

Sincerely,

To Current Teacher

Dear (**name**),

Now that the term is over and all the grades have been filed, I can take a minute to tell you how much I enjoyed (**name of class**). I didn't want to say this earlier, in case it looked like I was trying to "butter you up" or something, but I want you to know how much your class meant to me. I never knew how interesting (**subject**) could be. I learned a great deal, and had fun doing it. You're a wonderful teacher, with a real gift for (**kind of talent**). Thank you for everything. I hope you have a nice break before the next term starts.

Best wishes,

Attending Party

Dear (**name**),

I just wanted to thank you for coming to the (**occasion**) party I had the other (**day/night**). I think it went very well—everyone seems to have had a great time, including myself, and your being there was a big part of that. Thank you for adding your warmth and humor to the festivities; it wouldn't have been the same without you!

Love,

Wedding Gift

Dear (**name**),

(**Name of spouse**) and I were very touched by your lovely (**type of gift**). It was so nice of you to think of us, and to go out of your way to find such a wonderful gift. We can't wait to (**hang it on wall/put flowers in it, etc.**). Thank you very much for your generosity.

Warmly,

SEVEN

Relationships

This section is devoted to those times and occasions when you must make someone understand how serious or displeased you are with them or something they have done. It's also for those times when someone is acting displeased with you, and you don't know why.

Remember that confronting someone by way of a letter, if done properly, can be eloquent, tactful, and even fun! And it's a far more mature, responsible way to handle conflicts than any other method. That is, it's mature as long as you behave maturely: avoid name-calling, harsh language, and all other manner of histrionics. After all, the person who has deeply annoyed you is often completely unaware of their behavior and may not have acted intentionally. So, be polite. Besides, it'll make your reproaches all the more scathing!

To Parent: I'm an Adult

Dear (**Mother/Father**),

We've had some arguments before, on similar issues, but the most recent one really got me thinking. I've decided to write you a letter to let you know how I feel, so you can really absorb the words and not interrupt. First, I want you to know that I love you very much. You've been a wonderful (**mother/father**) to me in more ways than I can name. The problem between us is that you don't truly respect that I'm an adult. So many times you judge my decisions, or tell me what you think I should do instead of simply listening to my side of the situation.

I know you care about my welfare and that your intentions are good. But what you don't realize is that I'm entitled to make my decisions for myself. You may not agree with them, but you don't have to—it's not your life. You aren't raising me anymore. This doesn't mean that I don't value your opinion, but maybe you could wait until I've asked for it before giving it to me.

It's not my intention to hurt your feelings, and I hope I haven't done that. I just need to make my position very clear, because otherwise, if things go on as they have been, our relationship could be seriously damaged. I hope you can respect what I've said here, and know that I love and cherish you.

Love,

Ignore the Slanderous Gossip

Dear (**name**),

It's come to my attention that you've recently heard a particular story about me; namely, (**summarize story**). I'm writing to tell you that this is completely false. The person whom I believe started this tale is someone who is very angry at me for their own reasons. I intend to confront them and try to put an end to this. In the meantime, I am concerned about what lies others, like yourself, are being told about me. Before reaching a conclusion about me or this situation, please allow me the opportunity to speak to you about it in person.

Thank you,

Accusation of Spreading Gossip

Dear (**name**),

Some disturbing news has come to me lately. Apparently, you've been circulating a story among (**names of people/group**) that I (**summarize story**). As you well know, this ridiculous tale is a highly exaggerated and misinterpreted version of the actual events.

I expect you to make amends for this situation by contacting everyone you have spoken to about this matter and telling them that you had a few of your facts wrong. If you refuse to do this, I will be forced to tell those same people the true story, including why you felt you had to tell them lies about me. Then it will be *your* reputation that's in jeopardy.

I would also remind you, (**name**), that slander is illegal. If the gossip I've been hearing about doesn't clear up immediately, I will contact my attorney. If you rectify this situation yourself, however, no one will ever need to know that you intentionally sought to ruin my good name.

Signed,

Unappreciated "Advice"

Dear (**name**),

The more I've thought about what you said (**yesterday/last week, etc.**), the more I feel compelled to tell you that I didn't appreciate your "advice." I'm sure you think you were being a good friend by telling me what to do, but I think your remarks were inappropriate.

How I choose to conduct myself in the matter of (**issue**) is entirely my business. If you don't like my words or actions, you can say so—but do it in a less imperious way. Ask me to do something as a favor to you, to consider your feelings, and I may do it. But if you *tell* me to do something, because it's the "right" way, you're just being arrogant. You're not the arbiter of right and wrong, (**name**). You're just a person with a viewpoint, and if you express yourself in that manner, then I'll be much more willing to respect you and listen to you. I hope you can appreciate my feelings on this matter.

Sincerely,

Breaking a Promise

Dear (**name**),

Some time ago, you promised me that (**describe promise**). But recently, you've done just the opposite, choosing instead to (**describe breach of promise**).Try as I might, I can't understand why you would break your promise to me.

If you want to save our friendship, please call me and explain your side of the situation. I'm willing to try and understand your reasons, if you'll tell me what they are. But without any explanation, I'm too upset to continue thinking of you as a friend. Please get in touch soon.

Sincerely,

Chronic Lateness

Dear (**name**),

It isn't easy to bring this up with you, but we have a problem that I think needs to be addressed. For a long time now, every time we make a date you show up late. It's bad enough when you're late coming to my house, but when we're meeting somewhere and you leave me stranded, waiting for (**amount of time**) the way you did (**describe most recent situation**), it's just too much to take.

Being late is the same thing as saying "I have no respect for you. How I choose to spend my time is more important than inconveniencing you." I'm sure you don't mean it that way, but that's exactly the message you send. If it had happened only once or twice, I could understand. But you make a habit of being late. This has ruined our plans on (**several/a few**) occasions.

I want you to know that I can't keep being disappointed by you anymore. You'll have to learn to think of me as the one person who doesn't accept your lateness, and plan around that accordingly. Otherwise, there's just no way I can keep up our friendship.

Sincerely,

Not Returning Borrowed Items

Dear (**name**),

I have to admit that I wasn't completely honest with you the other day. When you asked to borrow my (**object**) and I said you couldn't because (**excuse**), that wasn't true. The real reason, (**name**), is that I simply don't trust you to return it. I'm sorry to sound harsh, but do you realize how many "borrowed" items I've never seen again? The list includes (**list items**).

I'm very glad we're friends, and I wouldn't want to offend you for the world. But until you earn my trust back by returning some of the items I've named, I can't lend you anything else. It just isn't right to take advantage of a friend that way.

Sincerely,

Insensitive Remarks

Dear (**name**),

I've been trying to avoid bringing this up, but the time has come to tell you that I don't enjoy your company as much as I used to. The problem is that you are increasingly making insensitive remarks about (**subject**). I'm sure you don't mean to be offensive, but I've told you several times that I don't think these remarks are as "funny" as you do. Yet, you still continue to make them.

Why aren't you more aware of my feelings? If you really are my friend, as you claim to be, you'll stop now that I've been frank with you. You're a nice person, and in many ways I like having you as my friend. But this one issue is bad enough that it's upsetting me to the point where I don't know if I can continue our friendship. In the future, please try to censor yourself so that we can remain friends. I hope you take this matter to heart.

Sincerely,

Oversensitivity

Dear (**name**),

I'm beginning to feel like I'm at my wit's end with you. It seems that every time we talk, even about something that should be simple and easy, you end up with your feelings hurt and hold me responsible. Your friendship is important to me, and I've gone out of my way to try to learn how to talk to you in a manner that won't offend you. But I feel like I have no option whatsoever; unless I continually praise you or agree with everything you say, you fly off the handle.

This is ridiculous. If you don't like me well enough to respect my honest opinions, you aren't really being a good friend. And if you also don't trust my affection for you enough to know that I can like you and still disagree with you—well, then you must not truly believe that I'm your friend. Please give this some thought and let me know if we can work this out. I'm not going to go through these dumb fights anymore.

Sincerely,

Rejecting an Apology

Dear (**name**),

Thank you for the apology you gave me regarding the (**describe circumstances**). I've been thinking about this quite extensively, and I have to say that I can't accept your apology.

What you did may not seem unforgivable to you, but I've decided that it is definitely unforgivable to me. I just can't get past it. Even if we tried to repair our relationship, I would never feel the same towards you again. I'm not saying this to hurt you or punish you, it's just that we've lost something that can't be regained, and there's no point pretending or postponing the inevitable. Good luck, and it's been nice knowing you.

Goodbye,

Demanding an Apology

Dear (**name**),

You know, there's an unresolved conflict that has been creating tension between us, and I've been waiting for you to address it—because frankly, that's your responsibility. But since you haven't brought it up, I guess I have to.

You know very well that I've been angry since (**describe incident**). I was extremely offended and hurt by that episode, and I've been waiting to hear some kind of an explanation or apology from you. However, none has been forthcoming.

Have you suddenly decided that our friendship is over, without letting me in on it? If that is not the case—if you think we are still friends—then you owe me an explanation. This is not going to go away by itself. If you want to preserve our friendship, please get in touch with me and tell me why (**incident**) happened, and what you have to say about it. If you do this, I might be able to forgive you and move on. If I don't hear from you, however, then I'll consider this friendship over.

Sincerely,

Why Have You Changed Towards Me?

Dear (**name**),

I've been noticing a real difference in your behavior towards me over the last few (**days/weeks, etc.**), and I've been hoping that you were just in a temporary bad mood or going through some kind of problem that wasn't connected to me. But after this much time has gone by, I have to conclude that your feelings have actually changed towards me.

I've racked my brain trying to think of something I might have done to upset you, but honestly, nothing has come to mind. Won't you tell me what the trouble is? If I've done something wrong, I'll gladly apologize.

Even if I can't fix it—even if you've just decided you don't want us to be close anymore—considering everything we've shared, the least you could do is give me some explanation. I deserve that much, don't I? Please get in touch and let me know what's happened between us.

Sincerely,

Ending a Romance

Dear (**name**),

Every time we've tried talking about our problems lately, we've gone around in circles and gotten nowhere. You seem awfully reluctant to hear what I'm saying, and I get the sense that you don't treat my thoughts and ideas seriously. That's why I'm writing this letter: I want to make some things very clear to you, without you interrupting or changing the subject.

For a long time, I've been very unhappy about (**explain problems**). I've done everything I can to change the situation, but nothing has worked, and I have to say that I just don't like the direction this relationship is going.

I see no way for us to fix this. (**Name**), I really think the time has come to put an end to this relationship. It just isn't working. The fact that I can't even talk with you about this face-to-face, but am forced to write a letter, is further proof that we don't communicate well.

Naturally I'll talk to you in person after you've read this, and you can tell me your reaction. But I have to tell you, I'm not open to continuing this relationship unless some pretty huge changes suddenly occur.

Sincerely,

To Ex-Spouse: Different Approaches to Child-Rearing

Dear (**name**),

(**Child's name**) came back here after (**his/her**) last visit with you, and told me about the incident regarding (**describe incident**). I would like to discuss this with you, as I have some major disagreements with how you handled this situation.

Personally, I've been handling similar situations in a totally different manner. I realize it isn't always easy for us to speak in person, but for (**child's**) sake, I hope we can try. We're both (**child's**) parents, and (**he/she**) is going to be influenced by both of our decisions and values. I think it would be in (**his/her**) best interest if we tried to agree on the ground rules. If each of us is teaching (**him/her**) different lessons, we're going to have a huge problem on our hands. Please call me soon so we can discuss this further. Thanks.

Sincerely,

Your Child Hurt Mine (Physical Injury)

Dear (**name**),

My (**son/daughter**) came home yesterday with (**describe injury**). At first (**he/she**) denied it was from a fight, but then (**he/she**) admitted that your (**son/daughter**) had caused the injury. Apparently, (**explain incident as you heard it**).

I know that kids will be kids, and sometimes fights happen. But I've always told (**son/daughter's name**) that it's not acceptable to express anger physically. This is a hard message to understand, especially when others are using physical force on you. Please have a talk with (**other child's name**) and ask (**him/her**) not to resort to violence in angry moments. Thank you.

Cordially,

Your Child Hurt Mine (Verbal Injury)

Dear (**name**),

My (**son/daughter**) came home yesterday in tears. When I asked what had happened, (**he/she**) said that your (**son/daughter**) had been teasing (**him/her**) about (**describe issue**). As you might know, (**issue**) is a real and somewhat sensitive problem for (**your child's name**).

Kids are often thoughtless without knowing it, and I'm sure your (**son/daughter**) didn't mean to be cruel. But it's important for children to understand how to accept differences and limitations in each other, without resorting to teasing. My child has been through enough hardship without having to deal with the additional burden of harsh teasing. Please have a talk with your (**son/daughter**), and encourage (**him/her**) to be more sensitive to my (**son/daughter**). Thank you.

Sincerely,

Your Child is a Bad Influence

Dear (**name**),

As you know, our children, (**names of children**), play together often. The other day I was startled to hear my child say (**describe language/concept, etc.**). I asked where (**he/she**) had heard this, and was told that it came from your (**son/daughter**).

I respect everyone's right to pursue their beliefs and to raise their children accordingly. But I have to say that these (**words/ideas**) are very different from what we teach my (**son/daughter**) in our own home.

I'm glad our children get along so nicely, and I don't want to put a stop to their friendship. But I would ask that you tell your (**son/daughter**) to be careful about speaking in this manner with children from different families. Please understand, I'm not passing judgment on your parenting skills; I'm merely trying to make sure that my (**son/daughter**) doesn't learn things that we don't believe (**he/she**) should be exposed to at this point in (**his/her**) life. Thank you for understanding.

Sincerely,

Substance Abuse

Dear (**name**),

I'm going to go out on a limb here, and say something you're probably not going to like. But I'm saying it only because I'm very worried about you. I've noticed that your (**drinking/drug use**) has increased a lot recently. I've also seen it start to affect your behavior in some frightening ways. For example, (**give examples of behavior**).

I wish you'd stop hurting yourself and hurting other people who rely on you and love you—the real you, not the disturbing person you turn into when you're (**drunk/high**). I've taken the liberty of finding out about an (**AA meeting/treatment center, etc.**) near you. Their phone number is (**number**), and they're located at (**address**). Please give them a call. And please don't be angry with me—I care about you way too much to watch you go through this without saying something.

Love,

Fighting Over a Will

Dear (**names**),

Ever since (**name of deceased**) died, we've been having a terrible time dealing with each other. I can't speak for all of you, but I know that the constant bickering and blaming is making my grief even worse, and has turned the whole episode into a complete nightmare. It's terrible that (**name of deceased**)'s will was (**vague/incomplete, etc.**), but there must be a way of handling it that doesn't cause so much heartache and anger.

I'd like to propose that we get together in one room, all (**number**) of us, and try to find a way of settling our differences in a way that would have made (**name of deceased**) proud. Otherwise, we may cause wounds to this family that will never be healed. Please get in touch with me soon, and tell me if you're willing to do as I've suggested.

Sincerely,

EIGHT

Neighbors

Most people have little contact with their neighbors, even though (geographically speaking) they are closer to us than anyone else. Sometimes, knowing what to say to a neighbor is simply a matter of common courtesy. Other times, issues can arise that are very difficult or awkward and which must be handled very carefully and with a great deal of thought. Keep in mind that, although you may not always socialize with your neighbors, they are the people with whom you most need to have peaceful relations. Strive for achieving that peace, and mutual respect, in all dealings with them.

Welcome to the Neighborhood

Dear New Neighbor,

Hello, and welcome to (**name of street/neighborhood**). (**I'm/We're**) your neighbor at (**address**), and I noticed that you recently moved into your new home. If (**I/we**) can be of any help to you while you are settling in, please let (**me/us**) know. Feel free to call (**me/us**) at (**your phone number**) or just drop by and knock on the door. I hope the transition moving here is going well for you. I look forward to meeting you in person.

Regards,

Request to Take Mail

Dear (**name**),

(**I/we**) will be gone on vacation for (**length of time**) starting on (**date**). (**I/We**) (**was/were**) wondering if (**I/we**) could ask you to take (**my/our**) mail and keep it until (**I/we**) return. I know this is a big favor to ask, and if you could do it, I'd be really grateful. I just don't want all the letters, magazines, etc. piling up and either getting lost or making it obvious that (**I/we**) are not home. (**I/we**) would be more than happy to return this favor the next time you go out of town. Please give (**me/us**) a call and let (**me/us**) know if this would be possible.

Thank you,

Congratulations on Property Improvement

Dear (**name**),

Every time I look out at your house, I'm struck by how nice it looks since you (**describe improvement**). I just wanted to congratulate you on a job well done, and thank you for doing something that benefits the whole neighborhood. We should all be trying to improve our homes in a way that makes the block look even more attractive. Maybe you'll inspire some other innovations, too!

Best,

Let's Begin a Community Project

Dear (**names**),

For some time, we've all been concerned about the problem with (**describe issue**) here in our neighborhood. So I have come up with a plan: what if we all spent some of our spare time trying to make the situation better? (**Describe your idea**).

If we all gave this a good effort, I think we'd see definite results—we could make this neighborhood a (**safer/more attractive, etc.**) place to live. What do you think? Please call me and give me your feedback. I look forward to hearing from you.

Regards,

Please Keep it Down

Dear (**name**),

For the past several (**days/weeks, etc**.) there's been a lot of loud (**music/ laughter, etc**.) coming from your (**apartment/house**). Unfortunately, sound carries very easily in this (**building/block/area**), and in (**my/our**) living room it sounds like you're right in the next room. This is somewhat disruptive during the day, but is especially bad at night. Do you think you could keep the volume down? (**I'm/We're**) sorry to ask this, because ideally you should be able to do what you like in your own home. But the noise level has really made (**my/our**) life unlivable here. I hope you understand and will be cooperative.

Thank you,

Rowdy Children

Dear (**name**),

I'm sorry to have to tell you this, but your children have been causing quite a disturbance lately. In the afternoons, when they're back from school, they (**describe disturbance**).

I would never suggest that a child's play time be cut short or too severely limited, but could you please explain to your kids that other people are affected by the noise that they make? Your neighbors (**on this block/in this building**) would be very appreciative.

Thank you,

Your Pet and My Lawn/Backyard

Dear (**name**),

I'm writing this note to let you know that I think there's been some trouble lately concerning your (**type of pet**) and my (**lawn/backyard, etc**.). Very often, I notice that (**describe damage**), and a few times I've seen your (**type of pet**) in the middle of (**describe offending act**). I'm not asking you to keep your pet a prisoner, but isn't there some way you can restrict his access to my property? I'd be very appreciative if you could solve this problem.

Thank you,

Your Dog's Barking

Dear (**name**),

One of the difficulties of owning a dog is that you have to try control its behavior to some extent. In the case of your dog (who is a very nice-looking and, I'm sure, wonderful pet) the issue that needs to be controlled is (**his/her/its**) barking. The noise level has become increasingly difficult to bear.

This is mildly annoying during the day, but it's a very serious problem at night when people need to sleep. It's impossible to completely "reason" with a dog, but it's not impossible to train (**he/she/it**). Please do what you can to see to it that (**he/she/it**) quiets down. Thank you very much.

Sincerely,

Assigned Parking Spaces

Dear (**name**),

As you know, parking around here is a bit difficult. That's why residents of this building rely on our assigned parking spaces. Lately, however, I've found that there have been other cars parked in my assigned space—and I've seen the owners of these cars coming out of your apartment. Perhaps you weren't aware that this particular space, (**describe location**), is assigned to me, but it is. I trust that in the future your visitors will not park there.

Thank you,

Threat to Take Action Against Neighbor

Dear (**name**),

For a long time, I and the other residents of this (**building/block**) have repeatedly asked you to (**describe problem**). This is a very serious problem, one that has had a strong negative impact on the whole (**building/block**). Yet you have ignored our requests, and have in fact become increasingly unpleasant every time we've approached you.

If you do not take immediate steps to rectify the situation, we will be forced to turn the matter over to the (**police/city/building manager, etc.**). I hope that we will not have to take such drastic measures and that you will comply with our requests.

Cordially,

Stolen Newspaper/Magazine

Dear (**name**),

I was wondering if you could help me with a problem that's come up lately. I subscribe to (**name of paper/magazine**), and it's routinely disappearing from my (**doorstep/mailbox**). Since the company assures me the (**paper/magazine**) is being faithfully delivered, I can only conclude that someone is stealing it.

As one of my nearest neighbors, perhaps you've seen who is doing this? I would really appreciate your help in putting a stop to this—if you see anyone coming up to my (**door/mailbox**), perhaps you could mention it to me. I will then report them to the police, as even something as seemingly minor as stealing a (**paper/magazine**) is a crime and carries heavy legal penalties.

Thank you for whatever assistance you can offer.

Sincerely,

Business Letters

Business letters serve two main purposes: first, they open the lines of communication to help you receive a desirable response, whether it's solving a problem, making arrangements, or seeking information; and second, they serve as official records of correspondence, so that you can strengthen your case, if need be, with physical proof.

It is vitally important that you follow a few simple rules when writing business letters. Doing so will allow you to capture the attention of the recipient and enable you to get what you want.

- Imagine yourself in the position of the recipient. You have a stack of mail on your desk and you don't have the time or, frankly, the inclination to read and answer each and every letter. Which do you respond to? The one that is addressed "To Whom It May Concern" and is sloppily written, or the one that is addressed to you personally, formatted neatly, and communicated respectfully and effectively?

- Today's business world is technologically advanced—virtually every type of office is computerized. But the people who run these offices are still very much human beings, so the traditional rules of effective letter writing, with a respectful human touch, still apply. In fact, it could be argued that in an increasingly automated world, it is even more important to emphasize our human qualities.

Where Should I Turn for Help?

When writing a letter to resolve a business matter, try to address it to the person with whom you have already been in contact. This person will usually be familiar with your situation; or if not, will probably be in a "hands-on" position, and will be able to expedite the matter most quickly.

If this fails, then and only then should you go a step higher—to that person's supervisor, or as the case may be, from a local to a regional or national office.

Other Guidelines:

• Get to the point! Respect the time of the recipient, and don't burden him or her with rambling or secondary background information. State your reason for writing in your first paragraph and stay on track.

• Always include facts that will help ease the recipient's task. For instance, if you are writing to a bank, mention your account number early so that he will not have to look it up.

• If you refer to other correspondence, mention those by date, check number, etc. Include copies whenever possible.

• Always be courteous! Even if you are frustrated or angry, maintaining a cool, calm approach will be beneficial to your situation.

The Format

Use the following as a guideline to writing an effective business letter:

Return address

Today's date

Name of recipient
Recipient's title
Name of company, organization, or institution
Street address or post office box
City, state, zip code

Opening salutation:

Body of letter

Conclusion

Closing salutation,

(allow four returns here)

Your signature
Your name
CC:
Enclosure:

Now Let's Discuss Each Step Specifically

Return Address. If you have pre-printed stationery, there is no need to include a return address at the top of your letter. However, if you do not, you must include this information at the very top (note: use only your address—your name still goes under your signature at the bottom). Never expect the recipient to find your address on the envelope, as it is often discarded upon opening.

Today's Date. Dating your letter, and dating it in a clear manner, is crucial. Always completely spell out the month. Use actual numbers for the date and year. For example, May 14, 2001.

Recipient's Name and Address. As stated above, the person to whom you are sending the letter will always choose to read and answer a letter addressed specifically to him before one with a generic greeting, for instance, "Dear Sir" or "Gentlemen."

So how do you find out the name of the best person to whom to address your letter? Just call the company or organization, explain the nature of your inquiry as concisely as possible to the receptionist, and ask for the name of the person to whom you should address the letter. If you are courteous and pleasant on the phone, most receptionists will be more than happy to give you this information. If you run into a problem, however, you should ask to speak to the receptionist's supervisor, or to someone in the Human Resources department.

If you know the person's title, then it will be helpful to include that under their name, but before their company name.

Opening Salutation. The easiest and most proper forms of salutations are simply "Dear Mr. (name)" for a man, and "Dear Ms. (name)" for a woman. For official titles, consult the "Forms of Address" glossary at the back of the book. Remember to never use a first name only (i.e., "Dear Lucia,") unless you already know the person well. Follow your greeting with a colon (i.e., Dear Mr. Baker:).

Body of the Letter. As you can see, the format page above is in "full-block" style, with all paragraphs flush left. Allow a full space between the paragraphs. All business letters should be typed or printed from a computer.

It is important to organize your thoughts carefully. The more coherent and structured your letter, the more impressive your statement. Be brief and get right to the point. Report facts accurately, without exaggeration or hyperbole. The recipient of your letter will appreciate your consideration of her time, as well as your respect for her intelligence. The letters in this book follow these rules. Use them as is, but learn from them at the same time.

Conclusion. You will notice that at the end of almost every sample business letter contained in this book, a "thank you" appears before the closing. It can be placed at the end of the body of the letter, or in a separate paragraph by itself. This show of gratitude is not only a sign of common decency, but also a subtle nudge towards a response that will ultimately benefit you. "Thank you for your assistance" not only expresses appreciation, it subtly rewards the recipient for the efforts she is about to make on your behalf.

Closing Salutation. Since this is a business letter, it is important that your closing reflect a respectful distance. Never assume anything more! Therefore, informal closings such as "Fondly," "Best regards," or "Yours truly" are inappropriate.

In nearly every case, a simple "Sincerely" will do just fine.

Always leave at least four line spaces for your signature, under which your name will appear typed. You may also include additional information below your name. It is appropriate, for instance, in a letter to the I.R.S. to include your social security number beneath your name.

CC. In the old days, "CC" stood for "carbon copies," and thus referred to those people to whom a copy of your letter would be sent. Although almost no one uses carbon copies anymore, the meaning of "CC" remains the same.

You may not use this that often. But if you deemed it wise to send a copy of your letter to another person, such as your attorney, your recipient's attorney, your physician, the recipient's supervisor, etc., you would place those names in list format after the "CC:"—remember your full colon!

Enclosure. In many cases, you will need to support your position with copies of original documents. For instance, if you are writing to a bank to dispute a charge on your statement, you will need to enclose a copy of that statement. You would then type "Enclosure: Statement for checking account number (**your account number**).

NINE

Education

There are two types of letters included within this chapter. The first batch are for those of you who have children in school and know how important it is to have a hand in your children's education. So many different situations arise at a child's school... a parent needs to know how to respond to them appropriately, in the way that is most likely to get good results. Alternatively, if you are in college, taking adult education courses, or are enrolled in any kind of continuing education program, you have probably found yourself needing to look out for your own rights. These programs are often are large, bureaucratic institutions where students and their paperwork can fall through cracks. The second set of letters will help your education go as smoothly as possible.

Suggesting a Field Trip

Dear (**name of teacher**):

I am very glad that (**name of your child**) has had so many opportunities, in your class, to go on fun and educational field trips. If I may, I would like to suggest a possible location for your next field trip.

For some time, my family has enjoyed visiting the (**museum/park/theater, etc**.). The last time I was there, I noticed that they have special group rates for schools and clubs. It occurred to me that (name of your child)'s class might like to visit, too. There's a great deal to see. (**Outline highlights of location**.)

If you decide that (**name of place**) would be a good site for an upcoming field trip, I would also be happy to volunteer my services as a parent chaperone. I am including a brochure from (**name of place**), which includes its rates and phone number.

Sincerely,

Suggesting a Fundraising Activity

Dear (**name of teacher**):

As a parent of a child in your (**number**) grade class, I've been aware of the recent discussions about the need to raise extra money. We all know that the bake sale has become rather stale (pardon the pun), and after giving it some thought, I've hit upon the idea of (**explain your idea**).

I think this is a very plausible and effective project. I'd

be happy to help organize the details and work with the other parents to make it a reality. I very much want to help (**name of school**) increase its income this year, and I believe this event could have the desired effect. Please contact me at (**your phone number**) and let me know what you think.

Sincerely,

To Teacher Harassing Your Child

Dear (**name of teacher**):

Over the last few (**days/weeks**), I've noticed that (**name of your child**) has come home from school looking less than happy. (**He/she**) has not wanted to discuss the issue, and I let it go for a while. But when it seemed that the sad moods were becoming a regular occurrence, I finally persuaded (**him/her**) to tell me what was going on.

It seems, (**name of teacher**), that (**name of your child**) is particularly unhappy with events that have been transpiring in your class. (**He/she**) feels that you are picking on (**him/her**) to an unusual degree.

I recognize the fact that children often exaggerate, and that a certain amount of a teacher's displeasure or discipline is regular and even called for in school. Nevertheless, I think it is important that we meet to discuss the situation. Please call me at (**your phone number**), so that we can set up a time to get together. Thank you.

Sincerely,

To Principal About Teacher's Harassment

Dear (**name of principal**):

An unfortunate situation has been developing recently in (**name of your child**)'s (**subject**) class with (**name of teacher**). After noticing (**name of your child**)'s unhappiness in school, I learned that (**name of teacher**) has apparently been submitting (**name of your child**) to an unusually high degree of public discipline and derogation. I have spoken directly to this teacher myself, and found the results less than satisfactory.

The activity has not lessened since my conference with (**name of teacher**), so I have no choice but to ask you to intervene. Please have a talk with (**him/her**). Or perhaps the three of us should get together. Either way, I'm requesting that you treat this matter with utmost urgency. Please don't hesitate to call me at (**your phone number**). Thank you.

Sincerely,

To Principal About Teacher's Poor Performance

Dear (**name of principal**):

I am writing to express my concern regarding (**name of teacher**), who teaches (**subject**) to my (**son/daughter**). I keep very involved in my child's schooling, and I've heard and seen some disturbing things lately.

I believe that (**name of teacher**) must be under some kind of unusual stress, for (**his/her**) performance has been slipping at an alarming rate. For example, (**give details**).

I've tried approaching (**teacher**) myself, but found (**him/her**) to be defensive and uncooperative. Please look into this matter and let me know what can be done. As a concerned parent, I need to be satisfied that (**name of your child**) is getting the proper education and attention (**he/she**) deserves. Thank you for your attention to this matter.

Sincerely,

School Bully Needs to be Stopped

Dear (**name of principal**):

It has come to my attention that one of the children at (**name of your child's school**) is causing problems for some of the other children. (**name of your child**), my (**son/daughter**) has told me that (**name of bully**) is routinely bullying the other children (**in class/on the playground, etc.**) Apparently, he has been (**give details**).

I urge you to contact (**name of bully**)'s parents and see what can be done about curbing his behavior. I don't like the idea of my (**son/daughter**) being intimidated—and even harmed—by this boy. I'm sure the other parents who know about him feel the same way. Please let me know what steps have been taken. I can be reached at (**your phone number**).

Sincerely,

Problem with Playground Supervision

Dear (**name of principal**):

After several discussions with my (**son/daughter**), (**name of your child**), I've come to the unavoidable conclusion that there isn't adequate supervision on the playground. Children are allowed to play very roughly with each other, with the biggest and strongest kids being far too physical with the others.

Children are naturally high-spirited and need to be watched, particularly when they're engaged in a physical activity. It seems that your current playground monitors are either too few in number or else woefully uninvolved in their jobs, for (**name of your child**) tells me that (**he/she**) has rarely seen these monitors step in to calm down the excessive behavior.

I'm sure you'll agree that no parent wants to see their children come home injured. Please let me know what steps will be taken to ensure a greater degree of care in playground supervision at (**name of school**). Thank you.

Sincerely,

Inquiring About Private School

Dear (**name of admissions officer**):

I am currently seeking an appropriate school for my (**child/children**). Your school has been highly recommended to me by (**name of friend/family member**), and I would like to inquire about the details of enrollment there.

Please send me a brochure from your institution, along with a current curriculum, if possible. I would also like to receive information regarding tuition, academic requirements for admission, and any other requisites for a successful application.

I look forward to hearing from you.

Sincerely,

Disputing a Grade

Dear (**name of professor/teacher**):

I received my report card today, and was startled to see that my grade in your (**subject**) class was (**a/an**) (**grade**). I believe this is an error, although I don't know on whose part. In fact, the grade I should have received is (**a/an**) (**grade**).

The rules you laid down for grading state very clearly that I should have received (**a/an**) (**grade**). I've enclosed a copy of your grading standards; as you can see, you stated that our grades would be broken down into the following percentages for each (**test/quiz/report, etc.**). I have also enclosed copies of my (**tests/quizzes/reports, etc.**), on which you wrote my grades. According to your own grading system, these assignments, weighted for their respective percentages, should have resulted in (**a/an**) (**grade**).

Please look into this matter, and see if perhaps an error was made in recording my grade for your class. If this is not an error, and indeed you intended to give me the lower grade, I would very much appreciate a conference with you to learn why. My phone number is (**your phone number**). Please call me to either set up a meeting or to let me know that my grade has been changed. Thank you for your time.

Sincerely,

Applying to a College or Graduate School

Dear (**name of admissions officer**):

I am interested in applying to (**name of school**)'s Department of (**subject**). I would like to request an application, tuition and fee information, and a form to apply for financial aid.

I would also appreciate literature on the (**subject**) program itself, especially in regards to program requirements and course offerings. I have enclosed my address and phone number. Thank you for your time.

Sincerely,

Requesting Transcripts

Dear (**name of registrar**):

This is a request for (**number**) copies of my official transcripts. I was a student at (**name of institution**) from (**year**) to (**year**), and my student identification number was (**number**). My social security number and birthdate are, respectively, (**number and date**).

I am requesting that these transcripts be official, sealed copies, and that they be sent directly to the schools to which I am applying for admission. Those schools, with their appropriate addresses are listed below: (**give list of names and addresses of schools**).

I understand that each transcript ccsts (**amount**), and am therefore enclosing a check for (**total amount**). Thank you for your assistance.

Sincerely,

Complaint to Department Chair About Instructor

Dear (**name of department chairman**):

I am a student currently enrolled in Professor (**name**)'s course, (**name and number of course**). For several weeks, many students in this class have been very concerned about the way in which this class is being run by Professor (**name**), and I thought you might be able to help.

The problem is that (**explain problem: professor is chronically late/unprepared/verbally abusive, etc.**) This behavior is ruining the class for a lot of us; some people I know have dropped out, and others just don't come as regularly as they did at first. No one feels comfortable approaching Professor (**name**) directly and asking (**him/her**) to change this problem, for obvious reasons; we don't want our grades to be penalized.

Is there something you can do about this? Please have a talk with Professor (**name**) as soon as possible, and try to resolve these issues. If you would like to speak to me, I can be reached at (**your phone number**). Thank you.

Sincerely,

Complaint to University Ombudsman

Dear (**name of ombudsman**):

I am a (**graduate/undergraduate**) student in the Department of (**subject**). This term I have had a very unfortunate experience with one particular course, (**name and number of course**), and its instructor, Professor (**name**). (**Explain problem briefly.**)

I felt this situation wasn't tolerable, and asked the department Chair, Professor (**name**), to intervene. (**He/she**) was extremely unhelpful, however; (**he/she**) said that there wasn't much that could be done, because (**explain reason given**). I'm not satisfied with this answer, and neither are several other students in Professor (**name**)'s class.

It's my understanding that you can arbitrate disputes between people, if all other ways have been tried. I've done what I can. Now I'd like you to intervene. If you would like to speak to me, I can be reached at (**your phone number**). Thank you.

Sincerely,

Reporting Sexual Harassment from Instructor

Dear (**name of department chairman**):

I am a student in Professor (**name**)'s course, (**name and number of course**). I'm writing this letter because I believe I am the victim of sexual harassment from this instructor, and I want to bring the matter to your attention.

For several (**weeks/months**) now, Professor (**name**) has been (**describe the harassing behavior—suggestive comments/gender-based insults/propositions, etc.**) I tried to be a good sport about it at first, but when it continued, I told Professor (**name**) that I was not comfortable with (**his/her**) behavior. (**He/she**) became very hostile to me at that time, and I now fear that I will be receiving a lower grade than I deserve.

Please look into this very serious situation. If you would like to speak to me, I can be reached at (**your phone number**). Thank you.

Sincerely,

Praise for a Valued Instructor

Dear (**name of department chairman**):

This is a letter of praise for one of the instructors in your department, Professor (**name**). I was a student in (**his/her**) course last term, (**name and number of class**). Very rarely have I ever had a teacher who showed so much skill at their craft. Professor (**name**) consistently (**describe exceptional behavior**).

If your department ever gives awards for outstanding teaching, I would hope you would consider Professor (**name**). (**He/she**) gave me an outstanding educational experience.

Sincerely,

Problems with Student Housing

Dear (**name of student housing officer**):

I am a resident of (**name of dorm/student apartments, etc.**) at (**your address**). I have lived here for (**length of time**), and during that time I have made several requests to the on-site manager, (**name of manager**) for (**describe request made—repairs/noise/vandalism, etc.**). Each time, I have been told that the problem would be taken care of, yet nothing ever seems to get done. I now feel your office should be made aware of these problems.

I recognize that we, as beneficiaries of low-cost student housing, are relatively fortunate members of the student body. But rent, no matter how low, means something significant to those of us who aren't wealthy. We pay monthly rent for these apartments, and we expect a satisfactory level of (**maintenance/noise/safety, etc.**) Please respond to me as soon as possible, and let me know what can be done to improve the conditions at (**address**). I look forward to hearing your response.

Sincerely,

Request for Financial Aid

Dear (**name of financial aid officer**):

My name is (**name**), and I am currently enrolled as a (**year: freshman, etc**.) in the Department of (**subject**). I am trying to find different methods of supporting myself to cover the ever-increasing costs of school fees and the cost of living, and it was suggested that I contact your office.

What kinds of loans or grants are available for a student in my year and field? Is there a list or catalog somewhere of available funds that I might consult? Please tell me how I might start working on finding alternative methods of funding my education. Appropriate information can be sent to (**your address**).

Sincerely,

From Parent: Dorm Security

To (**name of dormitory manager**):

I recently made a trip to (**name of school**) to visit my (**son/daughter**) who is a resident in (**name of dormitory**) dormitory. What I saw there made me uneasy regarding the safety of your student occupants. While there is some attempt made to ensure building security (**name security measures—locked front gate, etc**.), I nonetheless saw numerous opportunities for security breaches. (**Describe insecure aspects of dormitory—no guards/doors left open, etc**.)

Lest you think this is the paranoid rambling of an

over-protective parent, I would remind you that (**name of school**), while safer than downtown (**near-by city**), is not free of crime. Please contact me at (**your address and phone number**) to tell me what steps you will be taking to improve the security of (**name of dormitory**).

Sincerely,

Reporting a Classmate's Cheating

Dear (**name of professor**):

I am student in your (**name and number of course**). I have to tell you that I've seen a problem developing lately that angers me. As you know, our class is fairly large and not all of the students' desks can be visible to you at all times. I sit near (**name of cheater**) whom I have consistently seen cheating. Every single time we have had a quiz, (**he/she**) will (**describe method of cheating**).

I have hesitated to bring this to your attention, because I don't like the idea of being a "squealer." But I also resent the fact that I am working very hard to succeed in your class, and that someone else—someone who probably doesn't have the skills to make it on (**his/her**) own—is getting better scores than I am by being dishonest. If you plan on assigning our final grades using a curve-system, this is even worse. Then, this student's cheating will have a direct affect on my grade.

Naturally I would prefer that you not cite me as the source of your information. But please do whatever you can to put a stop to this flagrant dishonesty.

Sincerely,

Request Refund of Deposit for Dropped Class

Dear (**name of registrar officer**):

I enrolled this term in (**name and number of course**) and paid my per-unit fees as stipulated in the course catalog, for a total amount of (**amount**). However, due to circumstances beyond my control, I find that I have to drop this course.

It is my understanding that I am still within the (**number**)-week deadline for dropping a course and receiving a refund. I have enclosed my receipt for the fees I've paid, as well as copies of my paperwork for dropping the class. Please inform me if there are other steps I must take to receive my refund. You may send my refund check to (**your name and address**).

Sincerely,

TEN

Career

If ever strong letter writing skills are needed, it is here in the car category. Very seldom will you write a letter more important than one that concerns your job. A letter written to a supervisor or co-worker will reflect many things about your character, including your intelligence, attention to detail and your passion for the job. Always go over such letters with a fine tooth comb, checking for spelling, grammar and tone. Remember, your success with the company could eventually depend upon your ability to communicate effectively.

Restroom/Lunchroom Needs Maintenance

Dear (**name of office supervisor**):

I work in (**name of office/division**), and I regularly use the (**restroom/lunchroom**) (**on/in/at**) the (**describe location**). For some time, I've noticed that there is a problem that requires some attention. It seems that the room is always a mess. For instance (**give examples of mess: towels on floor/machines empty/plumbing leaks, etc.**).

Naturally, I realize that it's hard to keep a room ship shape when it has to serve so many people, and I'm sure there isn't sufficient staff to keep an eye on the (**restroom/lunchroom**) at all times. But this level of disarray is both unsanitary and unpleasant for those of us who depend on the facility, and I hope something can be done to fix the problem soon. Thank you for your attention to this matter.

Sincerely,

To Co-Worker: Let's Make Up

Dear (**name of co-worker**):

I know we've had some ups and downs here in the office over the last several (**weeks/months**), and that there has been a lot of friction between us. I think a lot of this friction is the result of miscommunication more than anything else, and I'd like to take this opportunity to apologize for my part in the problem.

I'd really like it if we could make an attempt to get along better, and I hope that we can start to communicate more effectively. Perhaps you and I could have lunch together one day and talk things over. We're going to be working together for a long time to come, and it would be better for both of us if we had a mutually beneficial relationship. Please let me know what you think.

Sincerely,

To Co-Worker: Please Keep it Down

Dear (**name of co-worker**):

We've got a pretty difficult setup here in the office, with all of us having to work in such close proximity to each other. I know it's hard to have to keep that in mind all the time, but I really do have to ask you to be a bit quieter. I don't mean to sound harsh about it, but you have a naturally (**loud speaking voice/loud laugh, etc.**), and you spend a lot of time (**on the phone/chatting with other employees, etc.**).

Please try to speak in a softer tone of voice. It's extremely hard for me to concentrate on my work with the volume level as high as it is. I appreciate your help on this matter, and I hope you understand that I don't mean to sound critical of you. I'm just trying to help create a more comfortable and productive atmosphere here in the office.

Sincerely,

To Co-Worker: Please Improve Performance

Dear (**name of co-worker**):

As you know, we work together on many projects and I see a lot of what you produce. Frankly, (**name**), I believe your work has been suffering as of late. Specifically, you (**describe weaknesses**). These mistakes and shortcomings of yours are making my job much harder than it needs to be, because I spend a lot of time fixing your errors. I shouldn't have to do this.

I'm sure you're ticked at me for saying this, and you probably don't think it's "my place." Technically, you might be right, but consider this: I'm telling this to you and you alone, and at the moment I have no intention of going over your head. I wouldn't bring it up if it weren't creating such a problem for me, but it is. I hope you can address my concerns, or else I will have to go over your head and tell our boss about the situation. I really would rather avoid all those nasty politics, so please try to do a better job.

Sincerely,

To Boss: Co-Worker's Performance

Dear (**name**):

I'm sorry to have to be writing this letter, but there's a problem here that I really think you need to know about. (**Name of employee**) has been doing pretty careless work, and it's been left to me to pick up (**his/her**) slack. For example (**give example**). I've spoken to (**name of employee**) about this situation, but (**he/she**) has refused to change (**his/her**) ways.

I realize that, because you're working at higher level, you aren't as immediately aware of the daily nuts-and-bolts of what (**he/she**) and I do. But believe me, it's a serious problem. My productivity is very badly affected by having to do (**his/her**) job as well as my own. Please have a word with (**him/her**) and see if this situation can be resolved.

Sincerely,

To Boss: Harassment by Co-Worker

Dear (**name of boss**):

For the past several weeks, (**name of employee**) has been making my working life here extremely unpleasant. (**He/she**) has made several inappropriate remarks which have made me very uncomfortable. For example, (**give example**).

I avoided the problem for some time, and then tried. speaking to (**him/her**) about it, but the problem has continued. Now I have no recourse left but to ask you to intervene. As you know, harassment of this kind is detrimental to the work environment and is also illegal. I hope you can have a word with (**employee's name**) and put a stop to it. If you have any further questions, please let me know. Thank you for your help.

Sincerely,

To the Boss's Boss: Poor Management Skills

Dear (**name of boss**):

I work in (**division/department**) for (**name of supervisor**). I'm writing this note because there is a problem with (**name of supervisor**) that I think you should know about. Although (**he/she**) is very (**list good qualities**), the problem lies in (**his/her**) management skills. Many of us who work for (**him/her**) are frequently disappointed in how (**he/she**) handles (**type of situation**). For example, (**give example**).

Obviously we can't approach (**him/her**) about this, because we don't want to jeopardize our jobs. Would you please have a talk with (**name of supervisor**)? I would appreciate it, and I know several of my colleagues would as well. Thank you for your time.

Sincerely,

Protesting Poor Evaluation

Dear (**name of boss**):

This is a formal letter of protest in response to the unfavorable evaluation I received from you on (**date**). A copy of this letter is going to (**name of boss's boss**), and to (**name of human resources officer**). I believe the review I received was unfair and inaccurate. The flaws you mentioned have never been pointed out to me in the past, and I heard no mention of the following exceptional achievements I have made in the past few (**weeks/months/years**). These achievements include: (**list overlooked achievements**).

It is my belief that (**name of immediate supervisor**) slanted my evaluation negatively to serve his own personal agenda, namely that (**describe agenda**). These are not valid reasons for negatively evaluating my entire performance. I believe that this evaluation is incorrect and unjustified.

Please respond to this protest and tell me what action will be taken regarding this incident.

Sincerely,

Office Equipment Needs Maintenance

Dear (**name of office manager**):

I don't know if anyone has called this to your attention, but the (**name of machine**) in (**location**) is not working properly. (**Describe the nature of the problem: broken copy machine/fax, etc.**) As you know, this (**name of machine**) is the only one in (**division/suite, etc.**) and is relied upon by (**number**) employees. I have mentioned this to (**name of boss**), but perhaps (**he/she**) hasn't had the time to inform you of the problem.

Please do what you can to either have this (**name of machine**) repaired or replaced. The working situation here has become very difficult, because without reliable equipment, our operations have had to slow down considerably.

Thank you for your attention to this matter.

Sincerely,

Apology to Superior for Impertinence

Dear (**name of superior**):

I just wanted to apologize for yesterday's incident when I said (**recount remark**). I now realize that my words were not appropriate to the situation. I have very strong feelings about (**issue that was being discussed**), and unfortunately I've been under a lot of stress lately, which makes it harder for me to filter my strong feelings through my common sense. Sometimes thoughtless words escape me, as they did yesterday, and I want you to know that I'm very sorry if I sounded impertinent or ungracious. I hope you understand that it wasn't intentional, and I won't repeat that behavior again.

Sincerely,

Please Chip In for Boss's Gift

Dear (**name of co-worker**):

As you know, I was chosen to select the gift for (**name of boss**)'s (**birthday/anniversary, etc.**). Well, after looking around, I purchased (**type of gift**) at (**name of store**) for a total of (**price**). Divided between the number of us here, that comes out to (**amount**) per person. Please stop by my desk (**today/tomorrow, etc.**) to give me your share of this gift. I also bought a card which is on my desk for you to sign.

Sincerely,

Request to See Personnel File

Dear (**name of human resources officer**):

As you know, I was recently (**fired/laid off/let go, etc.**). It is my understanding that my superiors submitted written evaluations of my performance before this decision was made, and that these evaluations are in my employee file. It is also my understanding that I am entitled to view this file.

This letter is a request to see my employee file. If I need to make an appointment to see the file in person, you may call me at (**your phone number**) so that we can arrange a time. If the file can be copied and sent to me, you can send it to (**your address**). I look forward to hearing from you either way.

Sincerely,

Request for Personal Computer Files

Dear (**name of human resources officer**):

My departure from (**name of company**) was, as you know, under forced conditions and I was given a very short amount of time to collect my belongings and leave. As such, I was unable to retrieve my own personal files from the computer at my desk. However, I am entitled to obtain copies of these files. Will you please return these to me in the form of a floppy disk? You can find these files on my computer in the (**describe directory/folder, etc.**).

These are not company-related files, but rather letters, notes to myself, and other personal documents that I wrote on my own time, during lunch. Please send them to (**your address**).

Sincerely,

Reporting Co-Worker's Dishonesty

Dear (**name of boss**):

I am sorry to have to write this, but I must tell you that a situation involving (**name of employee**) has arisen which I believe requires some attention. On several occasions, (**name of employee**) has taken credit for work done by others (**on this team/in this office, etc.**). I myself have been the victim of this behavior, and I spoke to (**name of employee**) about it. (**He/she**) pretended it had been an innocent oversight—but I noticed that it had happened on many other occasions.

Most recently, (**name of employee**) claimed to have (**type of accomplishment**) when I know for a fact that (**name of another employee**) deserves most of the credit. This other person was not there to hear the disservice done to (**him/her**), which is why I feel I must bring this to your attention myself. (**Name of employee**) is causing resentment and hostility within our group, because people do not like being elbowed aside and denied acknowledgment for good work they have done. (**Name of employee**) needs to be watched more carefully, and if possible, spoken to about this harmful dishonesty.

Sincerely,

Resignation Due to Persistent Office Problem

Dear (**name of boss**):

I regret to inform you that this is a letter of resignation. I have struggled with this decision for some time, but I believe it is the only course of action for me. As you know, I have been deeply concerned about (**issue**) for a number of months. Every time I have come to you with my concerns, you have placated me and offered me soothing words, but have never committed to taking any action to solve the problem. You have your own reasons for this, obviously, about which it is not my place to inquire. But the result has been that I've found that my ability to enjoy this job has completely disappeared. My job satisfaction is now zero, which makes this a good time to quit.

Naturally I will stay until you're able to find a replacement for me, if you so desire. I will also be glad to train that replacement, so that you can be assured of uninterrupted service. I bear no particular ill will towards you or this company; you clearly were doing what you thought was right. I am quitting not out of anger, but only because I need to have a job that I can enjoy and in which I can take pride.

Sincerely,

ELEVEN

Housing

This section is for those housing situations that require a well-written letter, whether it be the resolution of a maintenance problem, closing a sale, warning a tenant, or complaining about a neighbor.

Most housing issues can be divided into three categories: Buying or owning your own home, renting a house or apartment from a landlord, or renting a house or apartment as a landlord. All three situations will be addressed below.

Thanking a Real Estate Agent After a Sale

Dear (**name of agent**):

(**Name of spouse/significant other**) and I just wanted to take a moment to tell you how grateful we are for the wonderful way you handled the sale of our (**house/condominium, etc.**) I have to say it was a thorough pleasure dealing with you. You were a complete professional, and very charming from start to finish. We especially appreciated (**describe any special efforts**).

Thanks again for all of your hard work on our behalf. You've definitely earned your commission! If we know anyone who is thinking of selling a property in this area, we will definitely recommend them to you.

Sincerely,

Canceling a Relationship with a Real Estate Agent

Dear (**name of agent**):

After much discussion, (**name of spouse/significant other**) and I have decided that we need to take our (**house/condominium**) listing away from you. It's been (**length of time**) since we first listed with you, and the lack of results has been discouraging. I'm sure you're just as disappointed as we are, and we're certainly not blaming you. This may simply be a bad time to try to sell a property like ours. But we feel we have to try another realtor before we give up. Please let us know if any paperwork is required to cancel our listing with your office.

We're very appreciative of the effort you've put into this, and we thank you for all of your time and energy.

Sincerely,

To Building's Owner: Problems with Manager

Dear (**name of owner**):

I am a resident of (**your address**), a building of which you are the owner. As the owner, you are, I assume, the person responsible for selecting the on-site property manager. I thus feel that you should be made aware that (**name of manager**), our manager, is presenting problems which make (**him/her**) seem unfit to continue in this job.

The hours posted for the manager's presence are (**hours**). On several occasions, (**he/she**) has not been present during all of the specified hours and, when present, (**he/she**) does not respond efficiently to the concerns raised by tenants. For example (**give one or more examples**).

I hope you can address these concerns with (**name of manager**), and either see to it that (**he/she**) becomes more responsible, or that a new manager is hired in (**his/her**) place. Thank you for your attention to this matter.

Sincerely,

Request to Keep a Pet in Apartment

Dear (**name of manager/owner**):

I live in apartment (**number/letter**), and I've been a resident of this building for (**length of time**). I am writing to request permission to keep a small pet in the apartment. I know that my lease stipulates that no pets are allowed, but the (**type of animal**) I am getting is only (**height/weight**).

I am an experienced pet owner and I know how to care for this (**type of animal**) in such a way that (**he/she**) will not be a nuisance to the neighbors. I can guarantee you that the building and its residents will in no way be inconvenienced by this pet. If you have any other questions, please call me. Otherwise, I'd appreciate receiving your permission to bring (**type of animal**) home as soon as possible.

Sincerely,

Complaint About Movers

Dear (**name of manager/owner**):

I recently hired your moving company to help me move from (**address/location**) to (**new address/location**). Not having any prior experience with movers in this area, I relied on your advertisements and the questions answered by your staff when I made my initial inquiries. I have to say that I am seriously dissatisfied by the results of this move, and I do not believe your company lived up to its promise to (**quote promise or slogan**).

The movers in your employ (**describe problems—broken items/lost items/rude behavior/slowness, etc.**). I believe in giving people the benefit of the doubt, and I tried to be courteous and understanding of your workers at first. But by the end of the process I was truly frustrated with their performance. I have enclosed an itemized list of all the items that were (**lost/damaged/broken, etc.**) and I expect your company to make restitution immediately.

Please contact me at (**your phone number**) at your earliest convenience so that we may come to an agreement. If I don't hear from you within (**number of days/weeks**), I will be forced to take legal action.

Sincerely,

Requesting a Re-Assessment from Tax Assessor

Dear (**name of assessor**):

I pay taxes as a property owner, and I believe that I may be being improperly assessed for my property. I live at (**your address**), parcel (**assessor's map number**). I purchased this property on (**date**) for (**amount**), and have been assessed accordingly ever since. However, since that time I suspect that the value of my property has decreased. I base that suspicion on the prices I've seen paid for similar properties in my area, which are lower. I would like to request that my property be reassessed, to see if I qualify for a reduction in property tax. Please send any relevant materials to me at (**your address**), and inform me if there are any further steps I need to take.

Sincerely,

Threat to Withhold Rent

Dear (**name of manager/owner**):

As the (**manager/owner**) of this building, you are ultimately responsible for the quality and integrity of this property. For a number of (**weeks/months**), I have repeatedly asked you to fix the following problems in my apartment and in the common areas: (**describe problems: plumbing/peeling paint/heating**, **etc**.) I have seen no evidence that these problems are being fixed, nor have I received any assurance from you that repairs are forthcoming.

The standard of living in this building is becoming alarmingly low. By refusing to acknowledge the concerns of your tenants you are compounding the problem by demonstrating bad faith towards us. I am writing this letter as formal notification that if you do not take immediate steps to fix the problems listed above, I will withhold rent until such time as you do so. I am completely within my rights to do this, as any attorney will tell you.

I look forward to seeing these serious problems fixed in a timely manner.

Sincerely,

Problems with Doorman

Dear (**name of manager/owner**):

I'm sorry to report that I've had some recurring problems with (**name of doorman**), the doorman who works from (**time**) to (**time**) on (**days**). I've often found that he's not where he should be while on duty, and I've found that people come into the lobby and no one is there to greet, screen or direct them.

This building claims to protect its tenants from unwanted visitors, but that goal is merely a dream without the vigilance of a doorman. (**Name of doorman**) is too often away from his post, taking long breaks or doing whatever it is that he does. Also, my guests have complained on numerous occasions that (**name of doorman**) is not polite to them. These are problems that have a profound effect on the comfort of both residents and guests, and I hope that something can be done about it. Please keep me informed of what action you plan to take.

Sincerely,

Poor Building Maintenance

Dear (**name of manager/owner**):

I live in apartment (**number**), and I'm writing to let you know that the maintenance of certain aspects of this building is sadly lacking. Both I and my neighbors have experienced numerous problems with (**plumbing/heating/air conditioning, etc.**).

I know that several people have raised concerns regarding maintenance to you in the past, and that very little has been done. I am now placing this formal complaint on paper, and attaching a list of signatures I have collected from various residents in this building. We all pay regular rent, and we expect the structure and systems of this building to be kept in working order. If you do not address our concerns, we will report these problems and your negligence to the proper authorities. I expect to hear a response from you on this matter shortly.

Sincerely,

Reporting Drug Use

Dear (**name of manager/owner**):

I live in apartment (**number**), on the (**number**) floor. I'm writing this to alert you to what I believe to be a violation of drug laws in apartment (**number**). On several occasions (**describe drug use**).

I have also seen several different people coming at all hours of the day and night. I suspect that my neighbors are not only using drugs themselves, but possibly selling them as well. As you know, this could reflect very badly on this building and on you in particular. Also, it is creating a potentially dangerous environment for the rest of us. Please alert the proper authorities immediately, and see what can be done about having the tenants of apartment (**number**) evicted.

Sincerely,

TWELVE

Banking, Credit and Finance

In today's world, a good credit rating has taken on a role of major importance. It's a record of your financial reliability, and so it should be protected and carefully guarded.

This becomes even more important when you consider that, because they handle so many accounts and process so many transactions, banks and credit institutions will make mistakes. So it's up to you to make sure your statements are accurate.

If you notice a problem, don't shrug it off—write a letter to solve the problem. In these cases, a letter is far more powerful than a phone call, because it serves as a permanent record, and allows you to include copies of other materials, such as receipts and statements, to prove your case.

The following are examples of the most common banking, credit and financial situations.

Request for Services Information

Dear (**name of customer service representative**):

I have heard good things about (**name of bank**) from friends who bank with you, and I am intrigued by your recent advertisements that promise (**type of service**). I am considering leaving my current bank, and would like to request some information about what types of accounts and fees are available at your bank.

Please send me whatever brochures you have about checking, savings, money market accounts, cds, loans, and investment services. Also please tell me your hours and locations. Thank you very much.

Sincerely,

Please Reconsider Refusal of Credit

Dear (**name of credit manager**):

I recently applied for a (**name of credit card**) credit card, and received a reply from you saying that my request was denied. I am mystified by this decision, since I make a steady income and have good credit. I suspect that an error or oversight occurred, because I am absolutely positive that I'm in a sufficiently healthy financial position to receive credit with your company.

Please reconsider my application and let me know if you were able to reverse your previous decision. Thank you very much for your time.

Sincerely,

Wrong Charges on Credit Card

Dear (**name of credit manager**):

My name is (**your full name**) and my account number is (**your account number**). I noticed some discrepancies on my most recent statement from you. I've enclosed a copy of the statement and circled the errors so that you can see what I mean.

Specifically, there are charges here for purchases I never made, including: (**list charges**). I don't know what could account for this problem. It may be that someone else has been using my credit card number. If this is the case, I will have to cancel my account with you and start a new one, with a new number. In the meantime, however, please let me know what can be done about these incorrect charges. Obviously, they need to be removed from my account.

Sincerely,

Cancellation of Credit Card Without Notice

Dear (**name of credit manager**):

My name is (**your full name**) and my account number is (**your account number**). I attempted to use my (**name of card**) yesterday, and much to my dismay, the clerk at the (**establishment**) told me that the card had been canceled. Needless to say, this caught me completely by surprise.

More upsetting to me, however, is that you would cancel my card without even notifying me of this decision, thus setting me up to be humiliated when I tried using the card. This shows either gross negligence on the part of someone in your billing department, or, if it was intentional, it indicates that your company has no concept of how to treat your customers. I would like to have my account reinstated, and I would also like a written apology for the clumsy way this was handled.

Sincerely,

Poor Service From Bank Tellers

Dear (**name of bank manager**):

I have been a patron of (**name of bank**) since (**date**), and have usually found your customer service to be very satisfactory. However, I have noticed a certain decline in the past (**weeks/months**). The last time I was in your bank, I waited in line for an inordinate amount of time, due to the (**slowness of tellers/insufficient number of tellers on duty**).

When I was finally helped, my teller (**describe flaws: slowness/inefficiency/rudeness, etc.**). (**Give teller's name or physical description.**) After (**length of time**) as a patron of your bank, I would very much regret having to move my accounts elsewhere. But if your level of customer service does not return to its former high standard, that is exactly what I will be forced to do.

Sincerely,

Error on Bank Statement

Dear (**name of bank manager**):

I have a (**type of account**) at (**name of bank**), account number (**your account number**). On the most recent statement I received, I noticed a few errors in math—all in the bank's favor. I have enclosed a copy of the statement, and have circled the errors.

I find this very disturbing, because it makes me wonder if a trend of inaccuracy—or perhaps even dishonesty—is prevalent at your bank. Perhaps you think that an individual with a small total balance won't notice if someone skims pennies off their account? If so, you're mistaken. I expect not only to have the discrepancy re-credited to my account, but to also receive a written apology and a promise of no further "mistakes" on my statement.

Sincerely,

Requesting Record of Account Activity

Dear (**name of credit manager**):

I would like to request a full record of the activity on my (**name of credit card**) account for the past (**number**) months. My account number is (**your account number**). Because I use this card so often, I often have charges carry over from one month to the next. I have kept most of my monthly statements, but I find in going through my files that some are missing, and I therefore cannot trace some of the charges on the card.

The current total due on my most recent statement seems a bit excessive. But if I could see a full record of all the card activity over the last (**period of time**), I might be able to account for the apparent discrepancies. Please send this as soon as possible; I will not pay off the full amount due to you until I have verified that all charges are accurate.

Sincerely,

Protesting Insurance Hike: Second Driver

Dear (**name of insurance agent**):

I have a car insurance policy with (**name of company**), number (**policy number**). I recently informed you that I would be adding my (**child/spouse/partner, etc.**) to my policy, as (**he/she**) will occasionally be driving my car. The resultant hike in my premium was quite an unpleasant surprise, and I believe it is inaccurate.

Please take another look at the particulars I gave you regarding this situation. (**Name of second driver**)'s driving record is excellent, and (**he/she**) will not be using my vehicle frequently. Given these facts, it would seem that a more reasonable rise in premium would be in order. Please contact me if there is any problem, or if you have further questions about this change in my policy.

Sincerely,

ATM Deposit Never Credited

Dear (**name of bank manager**):

On (**day/date**) I deposited a check in the amount of (**amount**) through your automated teller machine. Even allowing for the normal amount of time it takes for a check to clear, that deposit should have shown up on my current statement. It did not. I am enclosing a copy of the receipt I received from the ATM at the time of the transaction.

I hope that the omission of this deposit from my recent statement is merely a simple oversight, and that the full amount will be credited to my account immediately. If there is any problem I should know about, please let me know as soon as possible.

Sincerely,

THIRTEEN

Community and Law

We all get caught up in the details of our personal lives, but sometimes we have to step back and remember that we really are a part of a larger community: our town, our school district, or sometimes, simply citizens who have rights and responsibilities.

This section deals with those times when you need to confront the issues of being part of a collective group. This includes instances when you must seek legal counsel, when you act as a community representative, or when you must either carry out or decline a civic obligation. Most people might be content to look at these issues and say "Oh, I'm just one person and the system is so big, nothing I can say or do will make a difference." This is far from true—a well-phrased letter in times like these can go a long way toward making your voice heard, your concerns resolved or your social position reaffirmed.

Complaint to City Council About Pollution

Dear (**name of councilman**):

I am a resident of (**city/neighborhood**), at (**your address**). Over the last several (**weeks/months**) I've noticed a continuing problem with pollution in (**name of area**). Specifically, (**describe locations and forms of pollution as well as reasons why this is harming your quality of life**).

This is a serious and unpleasant issue in this community, and I would encourage you to take whatever steps are feasible to reduce this problem. Perhaps our town needs to pass some stricter laws regulating (**type of pollution**). Thank you for your attention to this matter.

Sincerely,

Request to Remove Graffiti

Dear (**name of councilman**)

I am a resident of (**city/neighborhood**), at (**your address**). As you are the councilman for our district, I thought you should be aware that we have a significant problem with graffiti in our area. Specifically, the (**wall/building**) at (**location**) seems to be a favorite target for the local "artists."

It was repainted once, (**length of time**) ago, but the graffiti came right back. I don't know how the city can best combat this problem, but it definitely needs some attention. Those of us who live here feel that this disrespect for property is very disturbing, not to mention the sinister nature of some of the words and designs and the generally ugly appearance it gives to our streets. Please contact me and let me know what plans the city has, if any, for fighting this particular crime. The residents of district (**number**) are counting on you.

Sincerely,

Encouragement to Politician Running for Office

Dear (**name of politician**):

I just wanted to add my voice to the support I know you're receiving in your campaign to become our next (**name of office**)! I'm very impressed with your platform, particularly your positions on (**list issues**).

I've been waiting a long time to hear a candidate for this office say the things you've said. And beyond your words, I'm struck by your sincerity; you seem extremely committed to following through on the issues you've raised. I am very excited to see your name on our ticket, and I hope that (**date**) will bring you a victory! Good luck.

Sincerely,

Volunteering for Political Campaign

Dear (**name of campaign manager**):

I am a resident of (**your city, state**). I support (**name of candidate**)'s campaign for (**name of office**), and I'd like to get involved somehow.

I am qualified to (**list skills**). I would also be willing to simply go door-to-door, post signs, or do whatever else needs to be done during this important campaign. My current schedule is (**list free days and times**). Please call me at (**your phone number**) or write to me at (**your address**) and let me know how I can be of assistance.

Sincerely,

Request to Join Councilman's Task Force

Dear (**name of councilman**):

I was present at the community meeting you held last (**day**), and I would like to join the community task force you proposed to look into the matter of (**issue**). I have been a (**resident/business owner**) in this community for (**number of years**) and am thus extremely concerned about what goes on in my neighborhood.

I have many relationships with other residents and business owners in the area, and I could be of great service to the proposed task force. (**Describe your affiliations within the community.**) I hope to hear a favorable response from you soon. (**Name of community**) is very important to me, and I want to have a hand in deciding its future.

Thank you for your consideration.

Sincerely,

Reporting Use of Excessive Force

Dear (**name of police chief**):

I live at (**address**) in (**neighborhood/area**). I have lived here for (**length of time**), and have generally been pleased with the level of safety in our community. For the most part, given that crime cannot be one hundred percent eradicated, I think your police force is doing a fine job. But an event occurred the other day that I found most disturbing. I saw officers from your department publicly harassing someone in a manner that seemed excessive. (**Describe the incident, including date, place and time.**)

I realize that, as an observer, I wasn't informed of all the details. Perhaps this level of force was necessary. But I have to tell you that it made an extremely poor impression, and not just to me. Several passersby were shocked and stopped to watch what was going on. The (**man/woman**) being detained did not seem to be presenting a threat that was equal to the amount of harassment (**he/she**) was receiving. Please check into this matter and take any necessary steps to ensure that it does not happen again.

Sincerely,

Reporting Suspected Crime to Police

Dear (**name of desk sergeant**):

I live at (**your address**), and I believe a crime is being committed by one of my neighbors. On several occasions I have seen (**describe what you've seen/heard, etc.**).

(**Type of activity**) is illegal, and I am greatly concerned, not only for the people involved, but for the welfare of our neighborhood. Please let me know if you believe my suspicions are reasonable, and if you can address the issue in some way. We rely on you, as the guardians of our community, to put a stop to this sort of thing. I hope you are able to do so. If you need to contact me, I can be reached at (**your phone number**).

Sincerely,

To City Council Protesting Construction

Dear (**name of councilman**):

I am a resident of (**name of district**), at (**your address**). I am writing to tell you how strongly I disagree with the decision to begin construction on a (**type of structure**) at (**location**). I know this issue was under consideration for some time, and that you must have weighed all the pros and cons before approving the wishes of the developers. But it's possible that you are not aware of the serious repercussions that will befall our community if this construction goes as planned. (**Describe the problems—traffic/tearing down historical building, etc.**)

I would like you to reconsider you decision. If it is too late for that, then I would like to know what kind of feedback you solicited and received from actual residents of this neighborhood before giving the green light for these construction plans. Please respond to me on this matter. I would hope that, as our elected official, you are concerned with the opinions and the goodwill of the people who live and work in this community.

Thank you for your time.

Sincerely,

Character Witness for Defendant

Dear (**name of judge**),

I am writing this letter, as requested by (**name of attorney**), the attorney representing (**name of defendant**), as my proof of the quality of (**name of defendant's**) character. I have known (**name of defendant**) for (**number**) years in the capacity of (**type of relationship**). During that time, I have found (**him/her**) to be unfailing in (**his/her**) loyalty, kindness, and conscientious good will.

(**Describe activities and incidents in which defendant proved him/herself to be a good person**.)

I hope that you will take these remarks about (**his/her**) character into consideration when making your decision about (**name of defendant**)'s fate. Should you have any further questions, please do not hesitate to contact me at (**your address and phone number**).

Sincerely,

Reporting Poor Maintenance of City Infrastructure

Dear (**name of councilman**):

I am a resident of (**district/city**), at (**your address**). I am writing this letter to inform you that there is a serious problem with the infrastructure of our community. Specifically, there are (**describe problems—broken sidewalks/potholes/leaking water mains, etc.**) that are becoming an increasing cause for concern among local residents, and are making simple navigation of our (**streets/sidewalks**) very difficult.

In addition to functionality, the aesthetics of the neighborhood are also being affected. The worst problems are at (**location**), near the intersection of (**street and cross street**). I hope that your office can assist with this matter, and if not, that you can forward this letter to the appropriate office. Should you have any further questions, please contact me at (**your address and phone number**).

Sincerely,

Requesting Traffic Signals

Dear (**name of councilman**):

I am a resident of (**district/city**), at (**your address**). I am writing this letter to inform you that we have a pressing need for additional traffic signals in a section of our community. Specifically, the corner of (**street

and cross street) is a very dangerous intersection. In recent years this intersection has become more frequently used, owing to the (**describe reason**). With the advent of more traffic, especially during the rush hours, pedestrians can barely use the crosswalk there without fearing for their lives.

The current system of having only a stop sign at the intersection is insufficient. I have personally seen accidents, and dozens of near-accidents, at this intersection. Please do whatever your office can possibly do to place a traffic signal at this corner. The residents of (**name of community**) will be very grateful.

Sincerely,

Resignation from Local Committee

Dear (**name of committee chairperson**):

I am sorry that I must write you this letter, resigning my position as a member of the (**name of committee**). When I joined this committee (**length of time**) ago, I did so because I wanted to be an active, contributing member of this community, and to assist with its improvement and development. Since that time, however, I have been very frustrated with the progress—or rather, lack thereof—that our committee has made. At every meeting I've attended, personal politics and foot-dragging seem to have taken over and slowed down our agendas to a snail's pace. Without proper control of its members, our committee has, to my mind, degenerated into an ineffectual waste of time.

My civic inclinations have been severely dampened by this experience, and I'm sorry to say that I no longer feel that serving on this committee is doing either myself or our community any good. If you manage to somehow get things back on the right track, and restore a sense of discipline and purpose to the group's operations, please let me know. Until that time, however, I'm afraid you'll have to count me out.

Sincerely,

Request to Attorney for Rights After Being Fired

Dear (**name of attorney**):

On (**precise date**), I was fired from my job at (**name of company**). I believe that this firing was uncalled for and that the circumstances surrounding it are suspect. I want to learn if I have cause here for legal action.

I had worked at (**name of company**) for (**length of time**) and received favorable reviews on (**number**) occasions. My being fired, I am sure, is less a result of any poor performance on my part than (**describe why you believe you were fired**). I believe I have been wrongly terminated, and I would like to make an appointment to speak to you in person, to see what can be done about this. I look forward to hearing from you.

Sincerely,

Declining a Request to Help Out with a Function at Your Child's School

Dear (**name of function's coordinator**):

I'm sorry to have to tell you that I will not be able to help out with (**school name**)'s (**name of function**). Normally I would be quite happy to help, but my schedule is currently quite full.

I wish your teachers and volunteer staff the best of luck with this function. You have always done a wonderful job with these types of events in the past, and I'm sure this year will be no different. Thank you for considering me as an assistant, and please don't hesitate to ask again in the future.

Sincerely,

FOURTEEN

Press and Media

Just as there is much frustration with government these days, there is just as much frustration and mistrust of the media. But you need not feel so helpless. Write! You'll be surprised at what kinds of changes you can instigate by a timely, well-written letter.

The following samples will help you communicate your opinions to those in charge of television and radio stations, newspapers, and magazines. We'll also look at what to write when you find an advertisement to be particularly offensive.

Request for On-Air Rebuttal

Dear (**name of producer**):

I listened with great interest, and anger, to (**name of reporter**)'s editorial (**last night/last week**) on the subject of (**subject**). I find (**his/her**) views to be radically one-sided and completely at odds with my own experiences. (**He/she**) said nothing to acknowledge the important points on the other side of the debate, and thus left your (**viewers/listeners**) with no knowledge of the complexities of the issue.

I would like to fill that gap. I have a rebuttal prepared for (**name of reporter**)'s editorial, and I am requesting some air-time to present it. Your station, I believe, does have a policy that allows for such rebuttals. Please advise me of what requirements or stipulations must be met in order for this to happen. You may contact me at (**your address and phone number**).

Sincerely,

Protesting Cancellation of Comic Strip or Column

Dear (**name of editor**):

I have enjoyed subscribing to (**name of publication**) for several (**weeks/months/years**). For me, one of the highlights of your publication was the excellent (**name of strip/column**). I never failed to be entertained by (**name of creator/writer**)'s wonderful insights and (**comic situations/thoughtful writing**). I frequently would clip this section of the paper and (**hang it in my office/hang it on the refrigerator/send it to my friends**).

I must say that I'm extremely disappointed in the editorial decision you've made to stop running this (**strip/column**). I'd like you to reconsider your decision, and please tell (**name of cartoonist/writer**) how much I've appreciated (**his/her**) hard work. I hope to see (**his/her**) work return to your (**newspaper/magazine**) in the near future.

Sincerely,

Protest the Firing of a Reporter/DJ/Newscaster

Dear (**name of editor/programming director**):

I am a faithful (**reader/viewer/listener**) of your (**publication/program**), and I am writing to protest the recent firing of (**name of reporter/DJ/newscaster**). I understand that (**he/she**) was fired because of (**state reason**), but I find this to be an insufficient reason for such drastic action, and I'm certain that many of your other (**readers/viewers/listeners**) feel the same way.

(**Name of reporter/DJ/newscaster**) is a superb asset to your (**publication/program**). (**He/she**) is, in fact, one of the best in the field, in my opinion. I have never been disappointed in (**his/her**) work. (**He/she**) has a marvelous gift for (**describe good qualities**). I know our community depends on the wonderful (**writing/reporting/broad-**

casts) of (**name of reporter/DJ/newscaster**) to enhance their enjoyment of (**publication/show**).

I sincerely hope you will reconsider what I believe is a rash and unfairly punitive judgment, and re-hire (**name of reporter/DJ/newscaster**) immediately!

Sincerely,

Suggesting Story Idea to Newspaper or TV News

Dear (**name of editor/producer**):

I have been a faithful (**reader/viewer**) of your (**publication/news show**) for a number of (**months/years**). I respect the way you handle the news, and admire the tenacity and thoroughness you show in your reporting. That is why I would like your reporters to investigate an interesting story that is occurring here in (**name of community**). I believe it would make a valuable addition to your (**name of segment/section**). (**Provide details of story concisely, including the who, what, when, where and why.**)

This incident is having a profound impact on our community by (**brief description of impact**). I hope you and your excellent team of reporters will see fit to give this story the attention it deserves. Should you have any questions or desire further information, please don't hesitate to contact me at (**your address and phone number**).

Sincerely,

Correct an Inaccurate Report

Dear (**name of editor/producer**):

I have long been an admirer of your (**publication/news show**), and I rely on your usually excellent accuracy. Thus, I was surprised and dismayed to (**read/hear**) your report on (**issue**) in the (**date**) (**issue/episode**). Although correct in stating (**describe statements**), you were incorrect in stating that (**describe statements**).

In fact, (**describe accurate information**). I am in a position to know this because (**state qualification**). I trust you will amend your statements in the next (**issue/episode**) of your excellent (**publication/show**).

Sincerely,

Protest Consistent Bias in Reporting

Dear (**name of editor/producer**):

I have enjoyed your (**publication/program**) for (**length of time**), but I'm sorry to say that I'm not enjoying it as much as I used to. I've noticed over the last several (**weeks/months**) that a consistent bias has cropped up in your reporting. Time and again you slant your stories toward a (**liberal/conservative**) viewpoint—quite beyond the normal objectivity I used to expect from you. For example, (**give examples**).

In (**none/neither**) of these cases were your stated conclusions the only obvious ones. In fact, your considerable bias was forcing a particular "spin" on the stories that need not have been there at all. As an organ of public information, it is your job to provide thorough and accurate information—not to spout your own editorial biases. If this unfortunate trend doesn't reverse itself soon, I'm sorry to say that I will no longer be part of your (**readership/audience**).

Sincerely,

Respond to the Rescheduling of a TV Program

Dear (**name of programmer**):

I have been a fan of (**show's title**) since it began. I'm writing this letter to say that I think your station is making a big mistake by moving this show's time slot from (**time/day**) to (**time/day**). Your show, being about (**subject**), naturally has a large following among (**type of person/type of age group, etc.**).

This segment of your audience is not usually sitting in front of their TV sets at the new time to which you've moved this show; they're (**describe activity**). I think you'll find that, in this new time slot, (**show's title**) will falter and lose viewers. This would be very unfortunate, as I think it's one of the finest shows on television this season. Please reconsider your decision.

Sincerely,

Tasteless Advertising

Dear (**name of marketing director**):

I look forward to the end of the day as a time when I can relax, sit back and enjoy some entertaining television. The other night I was engaged in this pleasant activity, watching (**name of show**), when your commercial for (**name of product**) came on the air. I was not entertained. This particular commercial showed (**describe scenario**).

This is a crass, tasteless and completely unnecessary way to sell your product. (**Describe offensive matter**) has nothing to do with (**describe nature of product**), and I don't see why you'd choose to link them in this way. Your decision to do so has rubbed people's faces in something that many of us find ugly and upsetting. I, for one, will make sure *not* to buy (**name of product**) until this disturbing ad campaign is replaced with a more suitable one.

Sincerely,

FIFTEEN

Products

With the proliferation of home shopping networks, infomercials, and various other mail-order services, more of us are shopping from home than ever before. And with the "Information Superhighway," it appears this trend ***will only*** *increase.*

As such, the chances that a company will make a mistake on your purchase are high and getting higher. What's more, there are other situations that may not involve an error by a retailer, but where you still may need to write a letter. Maybe you've discovered that a product you purchased is missing a part, or that your favorite store does not stock a product you would like to purchase. Whatever the reason, a letter lets the retailer or manufacturer known, in no uncertain terms, what you desire.

Poor Instructions for Assembly

Dear (**name of customer service representative**):

I recently purchased a (**name of product**) from (**name of supplier**), and was very eager to assemble it at home. I was assured by the salesperson who helped me that the instructions were thorough and easy to follow. Actually, I found them to be neither. After struggling with the instructions for quite a while, I determined that they are crucially flawed.

In the section that states (**describe instruction**), there is a problem with (**describe problem**). As of this writing, I have been unable to successfully assemble my (**name of product**). I would like to receive either a more helpful set of instructions, or a manufacturer's refund for the full amount of the purchase. You may reach me at (**your address and phone number**).

Sincerely,

Wrong Parts Included

Dear (**name of customer service representative**):

I recently purchased a (**name of product, including model number**). When I took it home and began to assemble it, I discovered that the parts included did not match what was specified in the text or diagrams of the accompanying instructions. Whereas the instructions called for (**describe parts**), what I actually found in the box was (**describe what you found**).

I can only hope that this was an isolated error, and that you haven't actually been sending out thousands of units with the wrong parts! I would ask that you please send me, as fast as possible, the following parts: (**describe parts you need**). Please send them to (**your address and phone number**).

Sincerely,

Please Stock a Different Product

Dear (**name of store manager**):

I am a satisfied customer of (**name of store**), and have enjoyed shopping with you for (**length of time**). I generally have no complaints with (**name of store**), as I find it to be well-run and well-stocked. My only request is this: I've noticed for some time that the only brands of (**type of object**) you stock are (**name of brands**). I'm sure you have good reasons for choosing the brands you do, but I'd like to ask that you carry (**name of preferred brand**).

I've used the brands in your store, but I've found that (**name of preferred brand**) is far and away the better product. (**Describe reasons**). I'm sure that if your other customers had a chance to try (**name of preferred brand**), they'd like it too. Thank you for considering my request.

Sincerely,

Protesting Incorrect Charges for Returned Item

Dear (**name of store manager**):

On (**date**) I purchased (**item**) from your store in (**location**). I charged the purchase to my credit card. Later, I had to return (**item**) because (**reason**). At that time, I was assured that my account would be credited for the full price of the (**item**). I have just received my credit card statement, however, and I see that in fact I was not credited for the full amount. I have enclosed a copy of my original receipt for the item, as well as a copy of the credit card statement. As you can see, there is a discrepancy of (**amount**). I am sure this was an unintentional error, perhaps on the part of the salesperson who assisted me with the return. Please correct this mistake as soon as possible, and let me know when the correction has been made.

Sincerely,

Refund for Faulty Custom-Made Item

Dear (**name of store manager**):

When I first came to your establishment seeking a custom-made (**name of item**), it was because I had been led to believe that you did superior work. Your staff was indeed pleasant and helpful, but now that the (**name of item**) has been completed, I'm sorry to say that it isn't at all what I expected. Whereas I ordered (**describe specifications**), and went over these details at great length with (**name of staffer**), what I actually wound up receiving was (**describe discrepancies in finished product**).

There is no way I can use this item as it is, and I realize that you probably can't re-sell it. I would like to hear from you, to learn what can be done about this. Either alter the (**name of item**) to suit my needs, or provide a refund as soon as possible. Thank you for your attention to this matter.

Sincerely,

SIXTEEN

Services

Services differ from products in that you are paying for something intangible. The most common circumstances in this category include complaining about a service, disputing a charge, or praising someone who has performed a service for you. As usual, remember to be tactful, but firm. If you feel you've been wronged, stick to your guns and do not be satisfied until the problem has been corrected.

Car Repair Overcharge

Dear (**name of owner/manager of repair shop**):

I recently brought my (**make and model of car**) to your shop for (**type of repair**). The repair was accomplished adequately, but I must say that I am shocked by the amount of your bill, a copy of which is enclosed. Not only does this sum exceed the amount I was quoted by (**name of person who quoted you**), but it also far exceeds quotes I have gotten from some of your competitors, as well. I understand, naturally, that (**name of person who quoted you**) could only give me a "guesstimate" beforehand, but the size of the gap between that "guesstimate" and the actual final charge is too large to be ignored.

I would like an immediate explanation of these exorbitant charges, as well as a review of them; you should be able to reduce this price to something closer to the prices charged by (**names of competitors**), or at least, closer to the initial sum quoted by your own employee.

Sincerely,

Faulty Car Repair

Dear (**name of car repairman**):

On (**date**), I brought in my (**make and model**) for (**nature of repairs**). When I picked it up, I was told that the work was guaranteed for (**length of time**). First, I should say that (**describe repairs**) were done very well, as far as I can tell. However, the (**type of car part**) was not fixed. (**Describe the remaining problem.**)

Since your work is covered by a guarantee, and since it's only been (**amount of time**) since the work was done, I assume that there will be no problem with your fully repairing this problem, at no additional charge. Please contact me at (**your phone number**) to let me know when I might bring in the car.

Sincerely,

Poor Bus/Taxi Driver

Dear (**name of driver's supervisor**):

It was recently my misfortune to be a passenger in (**bus/taxi**) number (**number**), driven by (**name of driver**). I have never had such a harrowing experience in a (**bus/taxi**) in my life, and I believe you need to be apprised of how unacceptably this driver behaved. (**Describe bad behavior: reckless driving/foul language/mean to passengers, etc.**)

Commuting through traffic is distressing enough without having to handle the added worries caused by a thoughtless, irresponsible and unpleasant driver. Your company has an obligation to provide safe and comfortable transportation to the citizens of (**name of city**), and as long as (**name of driver**) is one of your staff, you will not be able to do so. Please see that (**he/she**) either changes (**his/her**) behavior immediately, or is terminated. I will not take another ride in one of your vehicles until I know this has occurred.

Sincerely,

Complaint to Dry Cleaner About Damaged Clothes

Dear (**name of owner/manager of dry cleaner**):

I recently brought my (**type of garment**) to (**name of dry cleaner**) to be cleaned. Your staff was friendly and efficient, I'm pleased to say, but the results of your work were far from pleasing. While it's true that you managed to completely remove the stain from my (**type of garment**), you also managed to completely destroy it. (**Describe the damage**).

I have looked into replacing this item, and have found a reasonably similar version of it at (**name of store**). Below is the charge slip for the new (**type of garment**); I expect you to fully compensate me for the cost. I still have the garment you ruined, and would be pleased to bring it in for your inspection, should you so desire. If you refuse to reimburse me, I will also be pleased to show this ruined mess to my attorney, not to mention your other customers. Please send the check to (**your address and phone number**). I look forward to hearing from you.

Sincerely,

Incorrect Charges on Phone Bill

Dear (**name of customer service representative**):

I recently received my phone bill for the month of (**month**), and was very surprised to note a total of (**amount**) for several long-distance phone calls that I am sure I did not make. I have enclosed a copy of my bill, with the disputed numbers highlighted.

I have ascertained that no one in my household—including friends, neighbors and the like—made any of these phone calls. Additionally, it is impossible that anyone else has had access to my phone. Please let me know what action will be taken to rectify this situation and to see that it does not happen again.

Sincerely,

Request Refund for Child's Camp

To (**name of camp director**):

As you know, I enrolled my (**son/daughter**), (**name of your child**), for the session at your camp beginning (**date**). I sent this payment on (**date**), and received confirmation from you that the payment had been received and processed, and that (**name of your child**) had been duly registered.

Unfortunately, it now seems that we will have to cancel these arrangements. (**An illness/a family emergency**) has come up, and (**name of your child**) will not be able to attend your camp this summer. (**He/she**) is very disappointed by this turn of events, as are we; your camp came highly recommended, and we were looking forward to our (**son/daughter**) having a memorable summer there. I would like to know how I go about obtaining a refund. Please contact me at (**your phone number**) or mail a check to (**your address**).

Sincerely,

Plumber/Electrician: Misleading Estimate

Dear (**name of plumber/electrician**):

On (**date**), I called your establishment to inquire about the cost of doing (**describe nature of job**). I was told that a free estimate could be given, and we duly made arrangements for that. When your representative, (**name of employee**), came to the house and assessed the job, he gave me an estimate of (**amount**). This estimate, however, was nowhere near what the job ultimately cost: (**total amount**).

(**Name of employee**) shrugged off my shock at the final bill and said only that estimates can be exceeded as necessary. I know this, of course; that's why they're called "estimates." But I don't believe that he was honest with me at the beginning. I have described the nature of the job and the details of the work done to several other (**plumbers/electricians**), all of whom have told me that your estimate was falsely low. I believe that you deliberately low-balled your estimate to ensure that I would hire you, and then increased the costs as the job went on. I consider this practice dishonest and unethical.

I expect you to honor the original estimate you gave me. If this does not occur, I will be forced to take legal action. Please send me a revised bill immediately.

Sincerely,

Plumber/Electrician: Faulty Work

Dear (**name of plumber/electrician**):

On (**date**), you came to my home to fix (**describe nature of problem**). At the completion of your work, the job seemed satisfactory; you submitted an invoice and I paid it. You also told me that the work was guaranteed for (**length of time**).

Today, however, I noticed that (**describe deterioration of work**). The guarantee period is nowhere near expiring; I have every right to expect your work to last at least (**length of time**) without problems of this magnitude! Please return to my home as soon as possible to repair this damage, as promised in the guarantee.

Sincerely,

Home Improvement Work Badly Done

Dear (**name of contractor**):

On (**date**), I employed your company to do (**nature of work**) at my home at (**your address**). I gave you a down payment at the time, with the understanding that the balance would be paid upon completion. As of today, (**date**), that work has been fully completed.

However, when (**name of supervisor**) told me "All finished," and came to collect the remainder of the payment, I was surprised. I had seen what point they were at just scant hours before, and couldn't believe that everything had been completed in that time. It turns out that I was right. The results that (**name of supervisor**) seemed to find "finished" are not at all my idea of what finished means. There are several problems with the work this team did: (**give detailed description of all problems**).

I will not pay the remaining balance of your company's fee until this work has been done to my satisfaction. If you do not believe that your workmen did an inferior job, I invite you to come over and see for yourself. I think you'll agree that my reaction is justified.

Sincerely,

Home Repair: Slovenly Workmen

Dear (**name of contractor**):

On (**date**), workmen from your company, (**name of company**), came to my home to (**describe nature of work**). They did a very good job, and I was satisfied. However, I noticed after they left that they did not clean up after themselves. (**Describe the mess.**) I subsequently had to spend several hours cleaning up this mess myself.

The life of any business depends in no small part on the desire of customers to become repeat customers, and on word of mouth. Although customer satisfaction does depend mostly on the quality of the work done, I have to say that another big consideration is how happy a customer is with the behavior of the specific workmen who come to their homes. In this case, I would not be able to say unequivocally that I would use your company again, nor could I recommend it to others without warning them to expect a big clean-up job.

If you're concerned with the reputation of your business, please have a word with the workers who came to my home. Any remedy you can think of, such as a partial credit or an offer of a discount on future work done at my home, would be much appreciated.

Sincerely,

Home Repair: Excellent Workmen

Dear (**name of contractor**):

Last week, I had workmen from your company come to my house to do (**describe nature of job**). Given my past experiences with workers in the home improvement area, I was not looking forward to this. Too often, I've dealt with dishonest or unfriendly people.

I have to say, however, that I am extremely pleased both with the workers who came, and with the quality of the job they produced. They were efficient, friendly, polite, and they thoroughly cleaned up after themselves when they were done. Best of all, my (**item repaired**) looks beautiful. I will be very happy to recommend (**name of company**) to anyone I know who might need similar work done.

Sincerely,

Retail Establishment: Poor Salesperson

Dear (**name of store manager**):

I came into your store, (**name of store**), on (**date**), in search of (**type of item**). I was able to locate and purchase this item, but not without a great deal of inconvenience and distress. This was due in large part to the salesperson who "helped" me. (**Name of salesperson**), (**give detailed description of salesperson's flawed behavior**).

The success of a retail establishment depends in no small part on the level of comfort your customers feel while in the store. This salesperson, looked at from that perspective, is a liability, not an asset, to your establishment. I am pleased with the product I purchased from you and would like to return to your store again, but I would not be eager to do so as long as that (**man/woman**) remains in your employ or retains (**his/her**) attitude. Please do whatever you can to correct (**his/her**) behavior or terminate (**him/her**).

Sincerely,

Retail Establishment: Good Salesperson

Dear (**name of manager**):

I just wanted to take a moment to tell you what an exceptional experience I had in your store last (**day/date**).

(**Name of salesperson**) was completely charming and very easy to deal with. This (**man/woman**) went to some lengths to help me find exactly what I was looking for. (**Describe salesperson's efforts**.)

Throughout our transaction, (**he/she**) was polite and friendly. This is not something I can say for all salespeople these days; many are lazy or downright rude. Your employee was a welcome change from that unhappy standard. I hope you can give (**him/her**) some recognition for (**his/her**) excellent work.

Sincerely,

Restaurant: Poor Service

Dear (**name of restaurant owner/manager**):

I dined in your restaurant last (**day/date**), and I would like to register a complaint with you about the service I received. Normally, a small tip is a sufficient message to send for poor service, but in this case the service was so bad that I feel it needs to be brought to your attention.

We were served by (**waiter/waitress—give name or physical description**). From the moment we sat down the trouble began. (**Describe problem: slow service/wrong food brought/surly manner, etc.**) The restaurant was not exceedingly crowded that night, and you seemed adequately staffed, so our server's shortcomings seem to be inexcusable.

A restaurant's reputation depends not only on the quality of food they serve—which in your case is excellent—but on the quality of service it delivers. Judged by these standards, I would have to say that your restaurant is not one that I would willingly return to, nor would I recommend it to others, unless you take steps to improve the behavior of the servers you employ.

Sincerely,

Restaurant: Good Service

Dear (**name of restaurant owner/manager**):

I have dined in your restaurant a number of times, and been waited on by several of your servers. I always hope, however, that I will be lucky enough to get (**name**) as my (**waiter/waitress**). Every time that (**name of server**) has waited on me, (**he/she**) has been unfailingly courteous and efficient. What's more, (**he/she**) has never gotten my order wrong—not once!—and has remembered me and always had time to exchange a few pleasantries. I've observed this even during the busiest times of day.

You're very fortunate to have (**name**) in your employ, and I hope there is some way you can give (**him/her**) some extra recognition for (**his/her**) wonderful service.

Sincerely,

Restaurant: Paying for Damaged Clothes

Dear (**name of restaurant owner/manager**):

(**Length of time**) ago, I dined at your restaurant and was waited on by a very pleasant young (**man/woman**). At the moment (**he/she**) brought our food, unfortunately, (**describe circumstances**) which resulted in (**his/her**) spilling one of the plates onto my lap. (**He/she**) was very apologetic and kind, and assured me that the restaurant would cover the cost of getting my clothes dry-cleaned.

To that end, I am enclosing a copy of the cleaning bill for the (**type of garment**) that was damaged that day. I have already paid this bill, and would like to receive a check made out to me for reimbursement. Incidentally, I hope that the (**waiter/waitress**) in question will not be punished for this accident, as it was not fully (**his/her**) fault. You may send the check to (**your address and phone number**). Again, no hard feelings.

Sincerely,

Post Office Needs More Staffers

Dear (**name of post office supervisor**):

I frequently use the branch of the post office located at (**location**), of which you are the supervisor. I'm writing to let you know that there is a serious problem with understaffing at this branch. I understand that a certain amount of waiting in line is to be expected. But for many (**weeks/months**) now, I have never been present when the wait was shorter than (**length of time**).

It is extremely frustrating and inefficient for working people to be standing in a long line, and to see a whole bank of windows with only two or three postal employees on duty. I don't know how you can rectify this, or if you can, given that funding for extra employees is usually pretty tight. But I would urge you to contact the proper authorities, and show them this letter. Your branch of the post office is the only one that services (**neighborhood**), and the public must rely on you to provide us with reasonable service.

Thank you for your attention to this matter.

Sincerely,

Make Sure Your Employees Can Speak English

Dear (**name of store owner/manager**):

I have been an occasional customer in your establishment for (**length of time**), and I am generally very pleased with the services and products you supply. Only one problem mars the experience: I have repeatedly found that your employees have difficulty speaking English, and this makes dealing with them extremely awkward.

I recognize that we live in a multicultural community, and I applaud your efforts to give jobs to recent immigrants. But surely there must be some immigrants out there who are studying English, and speak it with a good accent. The primary responsibility of any business is to provide adequate customer service, and when I have to squint, tilt my head, ask people to repeat themselves endlessly, and even resort to making them use charade-like hand gestures in order to understand what they are saying, then I would say that the level of service is somewhat lacking.

You run an otherwise fine (**type of business**) and I've never regretted my purchases there. I hope you can fix this one problem, for then you would have a flawless establishment in which anyone would be completely comfortable shopping. Perhaps you could urge your employees to enroll in an English as a second language course?

Sincerely,

Surly Behavior by Public Service Clerk

Dear (**name of supervisor**):

I recently had to visit the (**Post Office/Social Security Office, etc.**), to complete a (**type of transaction**). These types of errands are never "fun," but their level of pleasantness is almost entirely affected by the nature of the clerks who are there to help the public. I'm sorry to say that the person who helped me, (**name of employee**), was in fact no help at all, and was actually quite unnecessarily hostile. (**Describe the nature of the rudeness.**)

I sympathize with clerks who must stand on their feet all day and deal with the public, many of whom are probably not easy to deal with themselves. But that's not an excuse for becoming hostile and sarcastic with people who are not causing any trouble. Please have a word with this (**man/woman**) and instruct (**him/her**) to improve (**his/her**) pubic service skills. Thank you for your attention to this matter.

Sincerely,

Requesting Adoption Records

Dear (**name of supervisor**):

My name is (**your full name**), and I am writing to obtain some information regarding my adoption. I have contacted the agency that handled my adoption, and they directed me to your office. I would like to request access to whatever records of my adoption are currently in existence, and I am particularly interested in learning the names of my birth parents.

The information I have is as follows: I was born in (**city**) on (**date and year**). My adoptive parents are (**first and last names of each parent**), and my adoption was handled by (**name of agency**). I believe the hospital where I was delivered was (**name of hospital**), at (**location**). I hope this is sufficient information, as it is all I know. Please contact me at (**your address and phone number**) to inform me of how I may go about obtaining the records of my adoption.

Sincerely,

Inaccuracies in Utility Bill

Dear (**name of customer service representative**):

I was shocked when I received my last utility bill to note that the amount due was (**amount**). This sum is much greater than what I normally pay. I have not used any appliances to a sufficiently greater extent than in previous months, and do not understand the increase in (**gas/electrical**) power as you indicate on this bill.

I have not had any more people living in my home, nor have I purchased any new appliances. I am enclosing a copy of my present bill and my last one so that you may see the difference to which I'm referring, and I'd ask you to re-assess my power usage for this period. I believe that there has been an error in how you compute usage. Or perhaps your meter-reader simply misread my meter. Please contact me to inform me of your findings.

Sincerely,

Getting the Runaround from Customer Service

Dear (**name of supervisor**):

This is a letter of complaint regarding (**name of company**)'s methods for dealing with their customers. I have been a (**name of company**) customer for (**length of time**). I recently wanted to make an inquiry regarding (**describe nature of inquiry**). I found that this supposedly simple exercise was much more complicated than I realized.

(**Describe problems you encountered.**)

I am disgusted at how carelessly you treat your good customers. This entire, stupid operation took (**amount of time**) out of my day and resulted in nothing but frustration. I am submitting to you, (**name of supervisor**), as a supervisor in the Customer Service Department, my original question. I hope I can look forward to a speedy and thorough reply from you. If not, I'm sorry to say that (**company**) will no longer be receiving my business.

Sincerely,

Missing Refund

Dear (**name of supervisor**):

I am writing to inquire about the status of a refund check I was supposed to have received some time ago. On (**date**), I purchased (**item**) at your (**branch/location**). The item turned out to be the wrong (**kind/size/brand, etc.**) and so I returned it on (**date**). The salesperson who helped me, (**give name or physical description**), assured me that a refund check would be issued to me as soon as possible.

(**Length of time**) has passed, and no check has arrived. Please look into this situation. I expect to receive a refund check in the amount of (**amount**) as soon as possible. If there is any problem, please contact me at (**your phone number**).

Sincerely,

Rude Charity Volunteers

Dear (**name of fundraising supervisor**):

I received a phone call from your organization the other day, requesting a donation. Normally I enjoy making charitable contributions to your organization and others, but this year I was disturbed by what occurred. When I agreed to donate a small sum, your representative, (**name of representative**), sounded insulted, and tried to push me into donating more money. Unfortunately, I can't afford to donate grand sums to every charity that I find worthwhile, nor should I be expected to.

I reminded your volunteer that (**name of charity**) should count itself lucky to receive anything. No one is required to donate money; we do so as an act of kindness. If you expect to keep your charity afloat, I suggest you have a word with your volunteers. Explain to them that the *only* tone they should be taking with donors is one of gratitude.

Sincerely,

Threatening a Dishonest Merchant

Dear (**name of store owner/manager**):

I'm sure you recognize my name by now; I'm the person who has been attempting to reach a satisfactory conclusion with you regarding a purchase I made at (**name of establishment**). You have repeatedly ignored my requests, so I am now putting this in writing.

To summarize: on (**date**), I purchased (**item**) at your store. (**Describe what was wrong with the item.**) I sought to return it for (**refund/repair**), but was carelessly dismissed by your sales representatives. I then made my first attempt to contact you, as Manager, on (**date**), with no response. (**Describe subsequent attempts, if applicable.**)

As I am now stuck with a defective product and have received no attention from you, I must conclude that you are dishonest in your dealings with your customers. If you do not respond to this letter within seven days, I will register a formal complaint with our city's Chamber of Commerce and with the Better Business Bureau. You may contact me at (**your address and phone number**).

Sincerely,

SEVENTEEN

Travel and Accommodation

Taking a vacation or business trip can be quite complicated, especially if it involves travel to a foreign country. Finding out the best sightseeing spots, the best accommodations, disputing a hotel bill... there are a bundle of situations which can be made less complex with an appropriate letter.

So where do you turn? Travel agents, the office of tourism, and foreign embassies are always helpful—they want you to travel, to have a good time, and to spend your money there, so don't be afraid to ask them for help. And given the price of a long distance or international phone call, a letter is by far the most effective means of communicating. You will also find it helpful to write to hotels and other businesses for a variety of purposes.

Praise for Transport Employees

Dear (**name of supervisor**):

On (**date**), I was a passenger on (**flight/train/bus**) number (**number**) from (**departure location**) to (**destination**). I just wanted to take a moment to tell you how much I appreciated the efforts made by the staff of the (**plane/train/bus**) on the part of its passengers. Rarely have I experienced a staff so completely ready to be helpful and patient with people's needs. (**Describe their particular actions.**)

Long-distance travel is not usually a pleasant experience, but the presence of efficient and friendly staffers like the ones I encountered on your (**flight/train/bus**) made the trip a lot easier. I hope they can receive some extra recognition for their excellent work.

Sincerely,

Uncomfortable Airplane Trip

Dear (**name of customer service representative**):

On (**date**), I was a passenger on (**airline and flight number**) from (**departure location**) to (**destination**). I am writing this to let you know how thoroughly unsatisfactory this trip was in every respect. (**Describe problem with flight.**)

I realize that passengers in your coach class cannot expect the same level of comfort and service as passengers in first class. But do you realize that to us, your coach customers, tickets that cost upwards of (**amount**) are still expensive by our standards? We have every right to expect a minimal amount of comfort and service on your flights. If you cannot provide this to your customers, do not be surprised if they abandon you in favor of one of your competitors.

Sincerely,

Requesting Information About Destination

Dear (**name of tourist board employee**):

On (**date**), my family and I will be coming to (**city**) for a vacation. We have never been there before, and would like to receive some information about the city. First, we are a family of (**number**). We will be staying for (**length of time**) and are looking for accommodations in a (**type of class**) hotel. We would like to spend approximately (**amount**) per night, per room.

The ages of our group are (**give ages**). Do you have any brochures you could send us about appropriate activities or attractions in (**city**) geared toward these age groups? And finally, if you have tourists' maps of the area and a list of recommended restaurants that you could send, we would be very grateful. Please send whatever materials you have to (**your address**). Thank you for your time.

Sincerely,

Disputing Inaccurate Hotel Charges

Dear (**name of hotel manager**):

I was a guest at your hotel, (**name of hotel**), on (**dates**). When I checked out, I used my (**type of credit card**) to cover the charges. I have now received my new credit card statement, however, and I see some errors here on the bill. I am enclosing a copy of the statement, as well as the statement from your hotel, for your easy reference.

Note that I was charged (**amount**) by your hotel. This charge does not match the amount shown on my bill when I checked out. Please double-check your records, and credit my account for the appropriate amount. Thank you for your attention to this matter.

Sincerely,

Uncredited Hotel Cancellation

Dear (**name of hotel manager**):

On (**date**) I made a reservation at (**name of hotel**), under the name of (**name**), using my (**type of credit card**). I was told then that I would have to cancel this reservation by (**date**) in order to (**avoid being charged/receive full credit**). On (**date**), I had to cancel my trip to (**city**), and duly called your hotel to cancel my room reservation. The young (**man/woman**) I spoke to said there would be no problem, and canceled the reservation while I was on the phone.

Now I have received my latest credit card bill, and find

that I have been charged (**amount**). The name of the clerk who helped me is (**name of clerk**).

(**If you don't know the name of the clerk**): I do not know the name of the clerk who canceled my reservation, but I do know that I made that cancellation myself, and well before the deadline. Clearly the clerk made an error. I can prove that I made the cancellation phone call: enclosed is a copy of my phone bill for that month, with the call to (**hotel name**) highlighted.

Please credit my account immediately. If there is any problem, please call me at (**your number**).

Sincerely,

Dishonest Hotel Staff

Dear (**name of hotel manager**):

On (**dates**) I was a guest of your hotel, and stayed in room (**number**). When I returned home, I noticed that I was missing (**describe items missing**). The only person who had access to my room is the hotel maid. I hate to blame (**him/her**), but I do not know who else on your staff might be at fault. Have you had trouble recently with anyone in your employ? Have any other guests complained about missing items?

Please contact me as soon as possible and tell me what steps you can take to have my property returned to me, or to reimburse me for the missing items. My address and phone number are (**your address and phone number**).

Sincerely,

Praise for Hotel Staff

Dear (**name of hotel manager**):

I was a guest of your hotel from (**date**) to (**date**). I just wanted to let you know how very pleased I was with the staff of your hotel during my stay. Every day the room was cleaned perfectly, and the hotel maid and the desk staff were unfailingly charming and helpful. (**Describe any employees/actions with which you were especially pleased**.)

A stay away from home is much more pleasant when the hotel employees make everything go smoothly and comfortably. If I ever return to (**city**), I will be sure to stay in your hotel again. I will also recommend it to any friends of mine who may be traveling there. Thank you again for an excellent experience.

Sincerely,

Appendix

Forms of Address

GOVERNMENT

PERSON	ADDRESS	SALUTATION
U.S. President	The President The White House Washington, DC 20500	Dear Mr. President
former President	The Honorable John Smith Address	Dear Mr. Smith
Vice President	The Vice President Executive Office Building Washington, DC 20501	Dear Mr. Vice President
Cabinet members	The Honorable John (or Jane) Smith The Secretary of **cabinet** or The Postmaster General or The Attorney General Washington, DC	Dear Mr. (or Madam) Secretary

PERSON	ADDRESS	SALUTATION
Chief Justice	The Chief Justice The Supreme Court Washington, DC 20543	Dear Mr. Justice (or Dear Mr. Chief Justice)
Associate Justice	Mr. Justice Smith or Madam Justice Smith The Supreme Court Washington, DC 20543	Dear Mr. (or Madam) Justice
U.S. Senator	The Honorable John (or Jane) Smith United States Senate Washington, DC 20001	Dear Senator Smith
Speaker of the House	The Honorable John (or Jane) Smith Speaker of the House of Representatives United States Capitol Washington, DC 20001	Dear Mr. (or Madam) Speaker

PERSON	ADDRESS	SALUTATION
U.S. Representative	The Honorable John (or Jane) Smith United States House of Representatives Washington, DC 20001	Dear Mr. (or Mrs., Ms.) Smith
U.N. Representative	The Honorable John (or Jane) Smith U.S. Representative to the United Nations United Nations Plaza New York, NY 10017	Dear Mr. (or Madam) Ambassador
Ambassador	The Honorable John (or Jane) Smith Ambassador of the United States American Embassy Address	Dear Mr. (or Madam) Ambassador

PERSON	ADDRESS	SALUTATION
Consul General	The Honorable John (or Jane) Smith American Consul General Address	Dear Mr. (or Mrs., Ms.) Smith
Foreign Ambassador	His (or Her) Excellency John (or Jane) Jones The Ambassador of **country** Address	Excellency or Dear Mr. (or Madam) Ambassador
Secretary General of the U.N.	His (or Her) Excellency John (or Jane) Jones Secretary-General of the United Nations United Nations Plaza New York, NY 10017	Dear Mr. (or Madam) Secretary-General
Governor	The Honorable John (or Jane) Smith Governor of **state** State Capitol Address	Dear Governor Smith

PERSON	ADDRESS	SALUTATION
State legislators	The Honorable John (or Jane) Smith Address	Dear Mr. (or Mrs., Ms.) Smith
Judges	The Honorable John (or Jane) Smith Justice, Appellate Division Supreme Court of the State of **state** Address	Dear Judge Smith
Mayor	The Honorable John (or Jane) Smith His (or Her) Honor the Mayor City Hall Address	Dear Mayor Smith
City Council	The Honorable John (or Jane) Smith Councilman (or Councilwoman), City of **city** Address	Dear Mr. (or Mrs., Ms.) Smith

CLERGY

PERSON	ADDRESS	SALUTATION
The Pope	His Holiness, the Pope or His Holiness, Pope John Paul II Vatican City Rome, Italy	Your Holiness or Most Holy Father
Cardinals	His Eminence, John Cardinal Smith, Archbishop of **district** Address	Your Eminence or Dear Cardinal Smith
Bishops	The Most Reverend John Smith, Bishop (or Archbishop) of **district** Address	Your Excellency or Dear Bishop (Archbishop) Smith
Monsignor	The Right Reverend John Smith Monsignor Smith Address	Right Reverend Monsignor or Dear Monsignor Smith

PERSON	ADDRESS	SALUTATION
Priest	The Reverend John Smith Address	Reverend Father or Dear Father Smith
Brother	Brother John or Brother John Smith Address	Dear Brother John or Dear Brother
Sister	Sister Mary Jude Address	Dear Sister Mary Jude or Dear Sister
Protestant Clergy	The Reverend John Smith (or Jane Smith)	Dear Dr. (or Mr. or Ms.) Smith
Bishop (Episcopal)	The Right Reverend John Smith Bishop of **district** Address	Dear Bishop Smith
Rabbi	Rabbi Arthur (or Ruth) Simon Address	Dear Rabbi (or Dr.) Simon

MILITARY—Army, Air Force, Marines

PERSON	ADDRESS	SALUTATION
General of the Army	General John Smith U.S. Army (or Air Force or Marines) Address	Dear General Smith
Lieutenant General	General John Smith U.S. Army (or Air Force or Marines) Address	Dear General Smith
Brigadier General	General John Smith U.S. Army (or Air Force or Marines) Address	Dear General Smith
Lieutenant Colonel	Colonel John Smith U.S. Army (or Air Force or Marines) Address	Dear Colonel Smith
First Lieutenant	Lieutenant John Smith U.S. Army (or Air Force or Marines) Address	Dear Lieutenant Smith
Second Lieutenant All sergeants	Lieutenant John Smith U.S. Army (or Air Force or Marines) Address	Dear Lieutenant Smith

MILITARY—Navy, Coast Guard

PERSON	ADDRESS	SALUTATION
Fleet Admiral	Admiral John Smith U.S. Navy (or Coast Guard) Address	Dear Admiral Smith
Vice Admiral	Admiral John Smith U.S. Navy (or Coast Guard) Address	Dear Admiral Smith
Rear Admiral Lieutenant	Admiral John Smith U.S. Navy (or Coast Guard) Address	Dear Admiral Smith
Commander Lieutenant,	Commander John Smith U.S. Navy (or Coast Guard) Address	Dear Commander Smith
Junior Grade All chief petty officers	Lieutenant John Smith U.S. Navy (or Coast Guard) Address	Dear Lieutenant Smith

EDUCATION

PERSON	ADDRESS	SALUTATION
Dean of college or university	Dean John Smith name of college or university Address	Dear Dean Smith
President of college or university	Mr. John Smith, President name of college or university Address	Dear President Smith
President (with doctorate) of college or university	John Smith, Dr. of Law President, name of college or university Address	Dear Dr. Smith
Professor of college or university	Professor John Smith name of college or university Address	Dear Professor Smith
Professor (with doctorate) of college or university	Professor John Smith, Dr. of Law name of college or university Address	Dear Dr. Smith

JAICO PUBLISHING HOUSE

Elevate Your Life. Transform Your World.

ESTABLISHED IN 1946, Jaico Publishing House is home to world-transforming authors such as Sri Sri Paramahansa Yogananda, Osho, the Dalai Lama, Sri Sri Ravi Shankar, Sadhguru, Robin Sharma, Deepak Chopra, Jack Canfield, Eknath Easwaran, Devdutt Pattanaik, Khushwant Singh, John Maxwell, Brian Tracy, and Stephen Hawking.

Our late founder Mr. Jaman Shah first established Jaico as a book distribution company. Sensing that independence was around the corner, he aptly named his company Jaico ('Jai' means victory in Hindi). In order to service the significant demand for affordable books in a developing nation, Mr. Shah initiated Jaico's own publications. Jaico was India's first publisher of paperback books in the English language.

While self-help, religion and philosophy, mind/body/spirit, and business titles form the cornerstone of our non-fiction list, we publish an exciting range of travel, current affairs, biography, and popular science books as well. Our renewed focus on popular fiction is evident in our new titles by a host of fresh young talent from India and abroad. Jaico's recently established translations division translates selected English content into nine regional languages.

Jaico distributes its own titles. With its headquarters in Mumbai, Jaico has branches in Ahmedabad, Bangalore, Chennai, Delhi, Hyderabad, and Kolkata.

SINCE 1946